I0761213

Jasmin McGaughey is a Torres Strait Islander and African American author and editor. She has completed a Master of Writing, Editing and Publishing at the University of Queensland and a Master of Philosophy (in creative writing). She has spent time as a black&write! editor intern, was a winner of a 2019 Next Chapter Fellowship with The Wheeler Centre and won the 2021 Nakata Brophy Prize. She has written for *Overland*, *Kill Your Darlings*, *SBS Voices*, *Griffith Review* and was highly commended for the *ABR* Elizabeth Jolley Short Story Prize in 2020. Jasmin's passions have always been writing and reading and she is the proud author of Ash Barty's *Little Ash* series.

The Poet's Voice believes in the power of collective listening. Working in partnership with festivals and cultural organisations, founder Ellen Koshland and associate Nikki Anderson have curated large-scale events in beautiful venues, gathering people together to listen to poetry and prose on themes and topics both political and poetic.

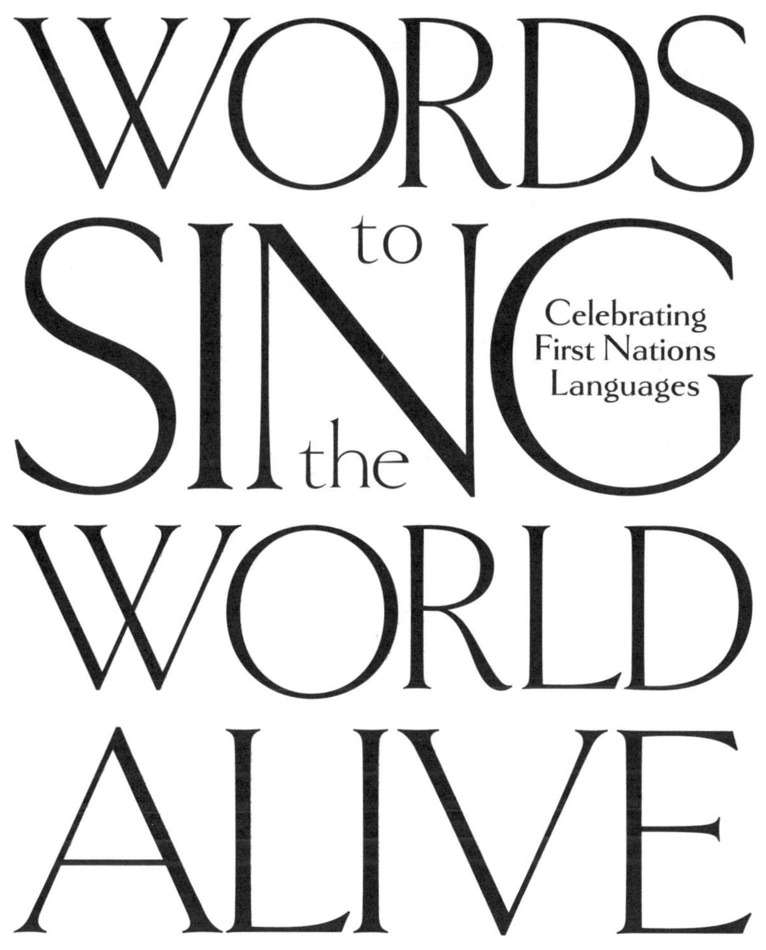

WORDS to SING the WORLD ALIVE

Celebrating First Nations Languages

Edited by

JASMIN McGAUGHEY and THE POET'S VOICE

UQP

First published 2024 by University of Queensland Press
PO Box 6042, St Lucia, Queensland 4067 Australia

uqp.com.au
reception@uqp.com.au

University of Queensland Press (UQP) acknowledges the Traditional Owners and their custodianship of the lands on which UQP operates. We pay our respects to their Ancestors and their descendants, who continue cultural and spiritual connections to Country. We recognise their valuable contributions to Australian and global society.

Cover design by Jenna Lee
Typeset in 12/16 pt Bembo Std by Post Pre-press Group, Brisbane
Printed in China by 1010 Printing International

University of Queensland Press is supported by the Queensland Government through Arts Queensland.

University of Queensland Press is assisted by the Australian Government through Creative Australia, its principal arts investment and advisory body.

A catalogue record for this book is available from the National Library of Australia.

ISBN 978 0 7022 6839 7 (pbk)
ISBN 978 0 7022 6952 3 (epdf)
ISBN 978 0 7022 6953 0 (epub)

University of Queensland Press uses papers that are natural, renewable and recyclable products made from wood grown in well-managed forests and other controlled sources. The logging and manufacturing processes conform to the environmental regulations of the country of origin.

Contents

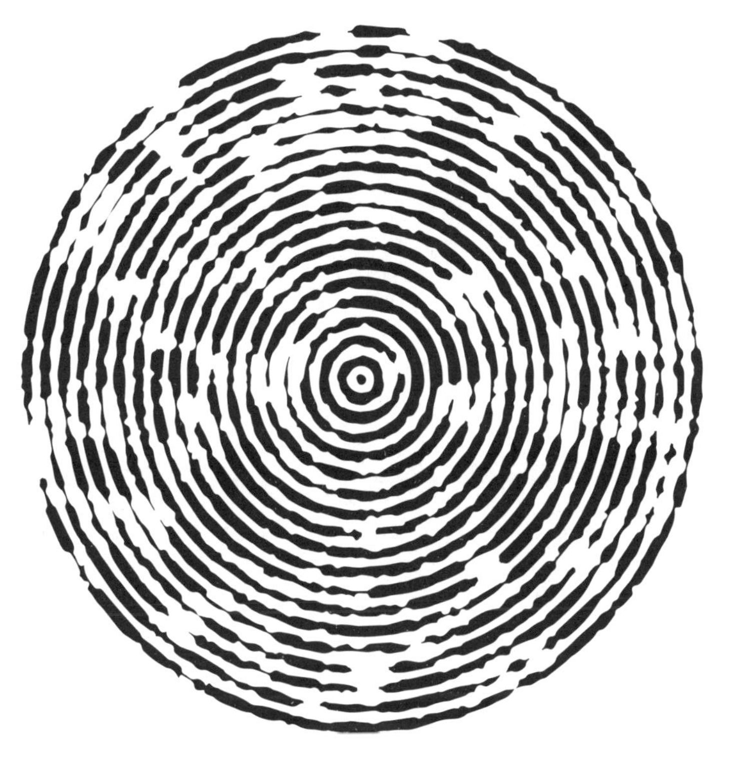

INTRODUCTIONS

Introduction
Jasmin McGaughey

I can only come to this topic – and write opening words for this book – from a personal stance. For everything here, in these pages, has been more than I can describe in English. Yet I have no other fully formed tongue for it.

Seeing and hearing language transfer across this space has been an experience I am grateful for. There has been pain, because I am reminded of what I don't know; panic, because I remember what I can know if I allow time and opportunity; but, overall, a joy for what has been shared. These pieces passed through many hands, and never once did they not make an impact.

There's something special in each of them. In Taneshia Atkinson's piece, I am given hope that our languages and our waters hold 'the perfect memory'. In Aunty Charmaine Papertalk Green's piece, I am pulled into memories. In Jazz Money's contribution, which gifted us this anthology's title, I see language in the landscape, and I see it in the bodies that occupy it. I see generational stories ebbing and flowing in Dan Bourchier's, Kim Scott's, Merinda Dutton's and Jared Thomas's pieces. Judy Watson and Otis Carmichael offer a family piece from two perspectives. Yasmin Smith's writing reminds me of those I am connected to. Mykaela Saunders brings me to Country I grew up close to. Sasha Kutabah Sarago and Adam Thompson make me think of how we care for that Country. Alice Skye's words weave my own craving for ancestral lands and seas.

Daniel Browning's, Nardi Simpson's, Aunty Lizzie (Elizabeth) Ellis's, Uncle Bruce Pascoe's and Uncle Paul Collis's words found homes here in these pages via a spoken-word event years ago, and it was their transcripts that initially captured me.

Ellen van Neerven, Jeanine Leane, Evelyn Araluen, Aunty Anita Heiss and Tara June Winch all contributed either an essay or a poem that had been previously published elsewhere. I remembered their words from earlier readings before this project and I believe they've helped frame the collection with beautiful and strong foundations.

Jenna Lee's and Timmah Ball's pieces were striking from the get-go, piercing in their truth-telling. Kirli Saunders, Samuel Wagan Watson, Vicki Couzens and Jacob Morris wove music in their words, and I heard it from the page. Cheryl Leavy, Claire G Coleman,

Bronwyn Bancroft and Kev Carmody were generous in how they gave parts of themselves to story for us, as readers, to learn. Karlie Noon made me think of starry nights and how my people learnt of the sky's power, and Jack Latimore offered something unique in the way he drew me into place and its atmosphere.

One of the most moving and touching aspects of this collection, for me, has been the amount of Torres Strait Islander voices. Aunty Rose Elu, Thomas Mayo, Terri Janke and Uncle Jimi Bani – mina koeyma eso to you all for this.

Some of these pieces have been seen or heard before, and some have been written especially for this collection. Each of them holds weight. In their piece, Amy Thunig writes about the Gamilaraay word Wuurri-lay – to give reciprocally – and I've felt that this collection, in part, is here to give pages and space to language. The First Languages of these lands and waters.

To any First Nations readers of this collection, I hope these words and moments shared bring you peace and learning like they did for me. A clarity that English, as the coloniser's tongue, often cannot bring to life. To non-Indigenous readers, I hope you are able to understand the generosity given here. And think in terms of circular reciprocity in how you respond. Like Aunty Rose asks in the opening piece: 'What will you do with this knowledge? How will this gift move on from you? Where will it return to?'

Introduction
Ellen Koshland

In this book forty First Nations voices share a word or phrase of significance to them. The contributors are writers, performers, lawyers, visual artists, academics and teachers, and include a number of Elders. I thank each of them for sharing with such generosity. These pages are a gifting of memories, poems, essays, provocations and reflections. Each word or phrase offered here speaks not just to a river or a yam, but to a way of thinking, to practices of listening, reciprocity, caring for resources and young people, transferring meaning and order.

Every language is much more than a set of words. It expresses a way of knowing the world. The language we use shapes our thoughts, our exchanges, our sense of culture and place. To encounter another language is often startling – it brings home to us that there is more than one way to make sense of our lives.

Over seven thousand languages exist in the world, but the words presented here hold particular resonance, for they are the original languages of this land, this ancient continent.

The words here sing the world alive. And not just with one reading, but each time. The vitality of these words is not surprising. They have sounded on this continent for thousands of years. They have been passed on from generation to generation. They have been sung and formed part of law and practice.

I marvel at the way these words connect, always. Language connecting to Country, language connecting to family, to ancestors. Language creating surprising conceptual connections – between a child and the tip of a tree, or the womb and the future, as in examples shared by Daniel Browning and Jazz Money.

In English, language often works to differentiate, to classify, to define, whereas here we are given life in constant relationality. We feel the depth of time-honoured culture and the way these words work in continual renewal.

The voices in this book speak from distinct places both within the whole continent and from the Torres Strait. We receive language from a flat land or a place of estuaries, from a creek bed or a wide river. This is precious today in a global world where homogenising tendencies threaten the particularities of local culture and tradition.

Many contributors draw attention to words forming on the tongue, inhabiting the breath, vibrating on the vocal cords. Each sounding becomes a singing, with words reclaiming our physical beings as well as our spiritual and cultural selves. We are reminded that there is also a language of the tides, a language of animals, a language of plant cycles and a language of the night.

Numerous personal accounts bring home the pain of language loss, the devastation of silencing and repression, and in turn make vivid the joy and empowerment of languages currently experiencing renewal.

Many leaders of that renewal feature here. Dan Bourchier, Amy Thunig and Daniel Browning in the media; Bronwyn Bancroft in children's literature; Charmaine Papertalk Green in education curriculum; Tara June Winch and Anita Heiss in innovative literature and poetry; Jacob Morris and Kim Scott in community; Vicki Couzens in visual art; Nardi Simpson in performance.

The evolution of this book has been a special experience. I first encountered the power of First Nations language being shared at two spoken-word events: the National Museum of Australia's *Songlines* exhibition, and the Victorian Premier's Literary Awards at The Wheeler Centre. On both occasions, First Nations guest speakers were invited to share an important word to them. The room rang out with evocations of time, landscape, gentleness and community, a new experience to many people there. Audience members felt privileged to be given these new understandings and this prompted the idea of a book that would encourage a celebration of First Nations languages more widely.

The gathering of forty diverse voices has involved many hours of dialogue and exchange across the country, all carried out by editor Jasmin McGaughey with her extraordinary thoughtfulness and care, assisted by Yasmin Smith at the University of Queensland Press (UQP). Aviva Tuffield and UQP have made the whole endeavour possible, once again enabling more First Nations authors to be read and considered.

A richer past is made available to us through these forty voices – and a richer future. What a gift this is in our world today. Words that ground us in the land we inhabit, but also a land we could aspire to inhabit.

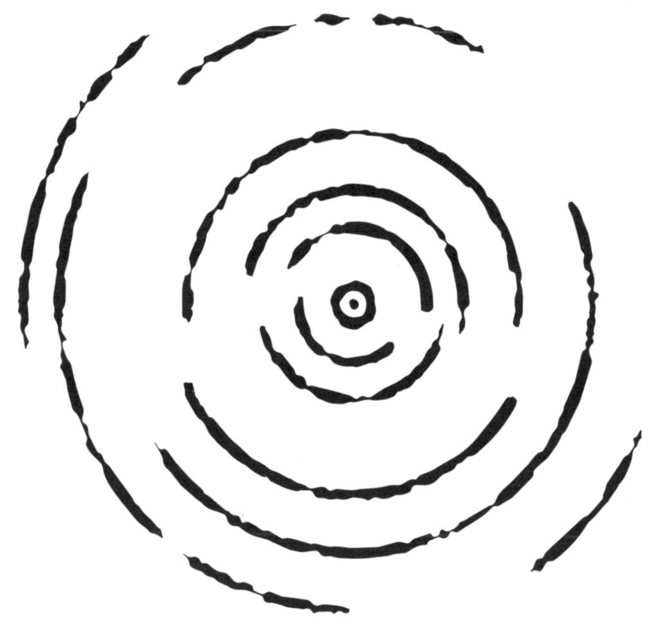

KURUSIPAGIZ

Aunty Rose Elu

AUNTY ROSE ELU is a Torres Strait Islander Elder whose decades-long work as an advocate for Torres Strait communities and climate change action saw her receive the 2021 Queensland Senior Australian of the Year Award. Aunty Rose was born on the low-lying island of Saibai in the Torres Strait. In 1949 her people moved to the tip of Australia, to an island now known as Seisia, which was given to her father and his brothers by the Aboriginal people of Cape York, Queensland.

Kurusipagiz is a Kalaw Lagaw Ya word from the top-western Torres Strait Islands – it's a Saibai language word. This word is important to me as it applies to interpreting, observing, understanding, accepting and responding. It means you are listening, or you have listened.

If ever I am presenting or participating in discussions relating to my culture, traditions and heritage, I must listen and I must ask my audience to listen. I give myself wholly to share what I have learnt through my years of growing up, of learning cultural knowledge taught to me by my parents and extended families. It's through listening carefully and embracing listening and knowledge firmly that I am able to talk freely and teach others.

Kurusipagiz asks us to listen without interrupting. It asks us to listen before making our own judgements or responses.

As I grew up, I always had to listen very carefully before I intervened so I could have a better understanding of what was being taught to me. For example, cultural advice was given to me when I became of age. This counsel was given to help me with my life's purpose and my career, and to advise on what life would bring to me. It taught me how I could face the world, the things I would have to do and how I could do them properly. Over and over again, this knowledge was given to me. I was taught about the cultural differences I would see, because I have my own culture and a Western culture that I must live in. How could I bring my culture to this Western life without understanding my world and the worlds of others?

I come from a chieftain clan, so there are also cultural advisors, and there's a lot of work – a lot of listening – that needs to be done to be a cultural advisor. In my culture, you learn not to do things in a rush and risk making mistakes.

I've learnt to never interrupt when someone is talking. Or else by the time we give the answer it's often not the true answer. Define it first so you can come with understanding to the conversation. Translating language is difficult and is part of this discussion. Sentence structures vary between my language and English. That's why I'll listen carefully. Because I must interpret before I answer.

If you really listen carefully, you enjoy the learning. There's always questions that come and things you must clarify, but you know you are doing the right thing, that you are on the right path, when you listen.

I want you, as readers, to really listen carefully. Are you taking everything into account? I want you to listen intently so you can have a better understanding of what's on the table. And more than that, I want you to understand what you're witnessing. One example I think of is Sorry Business. Why is this business so important to many Indigenous people? If you are non-Indigenous and from a Western background, look at your own forms of grieving. How do you perform your grieving processes? How do we? Why might Sorry Business go on for longer than what the Western world dictates to be normal? There are explanations that come with each step of Sorry Business.

If you do listen to something important, or even a common discussion, make sure you don't interrupt too quickly. You wait until it's finished.

My parents used to say, 'When you're listening, wait until the last person speaks and the last word is spoken. That will give you the answer to how you will reply. That will give you a clearer interpretation of the whole thing. If you don't understand, you listen still and ask questions after.'

Through my journey, I've experienced people talking too fast, too eager to get a response out. They are so adamant that they want to say something that they forget to listen. When you listen, you can then embrace that knowledge that has been given to you, because it is with you. It gives you purpose when you embrace listening. You will do the right thing by that knowledge.

Many times, people have come up to me to thank me for speaking and sharing knowledge. I know then that I have been able to get them to listen carefully to my words. It means that they have understood me.

What you understand depends on how you perceive my words, which depends on how well you listen. That's why I chose this word.

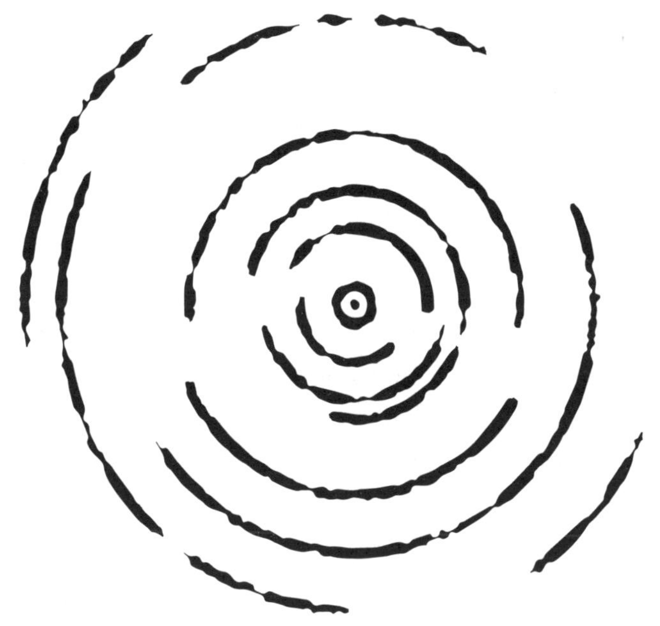

GIYIRA

Jazz Money

JAZZ MONEY is a Wiradjuri poet and artist whose practice is centred around poetics to produce works that encompass installation, digital, performance, film and print. Their writing and art has been widely presented, performed and published nationally and internationally. Jazz has released two poetry collections, *mark the dawn*, winner of the Quentin Bryce Award in 2024, and *how to make a basket*, winner of the David Unaipon Award in 2020.

the dawn sent you darling one
that's when we knew
golden light lit up with your laughing
we stepped together then
and felt Country sing back to your beating heart
leading us down far glowing path
all the way forward
all the way back

—

The yellow cover is getting soft on my Wiradjuri dictionary from constant use. Sometimes this heavy book lives in the urgent stack of papers that decorates my desk, other times it travels to the place next to my bed for lazy browsing. On any day it may be found by the comfy faded chair, upon the wooden dining table, among the ephemera in the hallway where things go to get lost. It is a book that does not get dusty on the shelf: it has the range of a migratory bird around the humble ridges that make up this apartment.

The thin papers reward a wandering eye, always a new pathway for the mind to travel. The pages are a map of bold, italic, underlined. Latin alphabet describing Wiradjuri words into English, English words into Wiradjuri, and all the words of Country that don't fit neatly into the confines of the coloniser's world. This is a language alive in the mouth, transcribed to the written. Compiled intricate, esoteric and huge by Dr Uncle Stan Grant Senior and Dr John Rudder, these same pages are love-worn by Koories across the South-East.

But it's on the tongue where this language sings the world alive. Any one word can feel like a story, a narrative in small syllables. An arrangement of breath where my body and spirit inhabit. The muscles on my face are clunky, learning the shapes carved by rivers, known by sky. I was raised in English, and so I am finding my way back to myself through this sun-warmed language. Journeys through time, forward and back, held by language, held by Country.

This is the world where I want my small ones to feel held. As natural as their dancing bodies, as their laughing bellies. A language that flows as powerful as the waters that shape our river-bound homeland.

We haven't made these babies yet. Our love will not make them manifest without long conversations, the help of other bodies and fluids we do not produce. For now, they are future beings, with star trails stretched against our skies as we wait for every step in this lasting choreography to come together.

These potential lives illuminate our faces sometimes when I turn the pages of the dictionary, considering possible names for these new ones yet to come here. Will we name them for bird, for blossom, for sunrise? Bilirr, yurali, yiray. Whoever they are, the first name they hear will be a sound known since the first sunrise. A language that always has been.

These are the giyira questions. Womb question, future question.

In Wiradjuri, womb and future share a word: giyira. Big dawn-filled word. A philosophy in practice of care, of knowing, of science, of time. This is the world I want my babies to enter, one that knows the weight of their breath. The worth of their breath. What will that world be, bubby-one? Safer and slower maybe. A world where the wrongs of now are in retreat.

Can we dream up the world we want for our next ones? Can we sing it together?

The future I want for my babies is one with sovereignty held by First Nations peoples across the world, self-determined and determined by care. A future with the climate crisis reversed, the bush in bloom. A world that will not demand gender or sexuality, not be shaped by capitalism and imperialism. A time not so far away.

Womb question, future question.

Can we return to the elegance of giyira? To understand that our inheritance is our future, that care is collective. Held in giyira is a philosophy of time, one that stretches all the way forward and all the way back. An understanding of science, an integrating of biology, physics, sociology. These are old knowledges that hold the world together, giyira way.

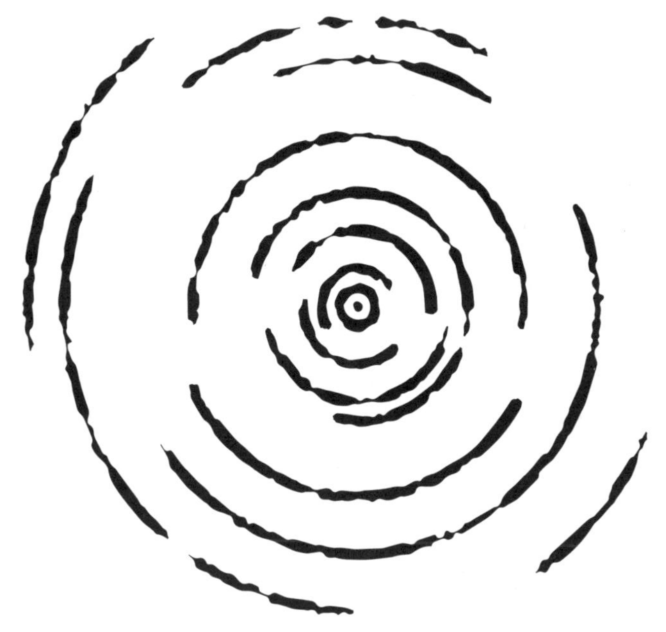

NGUMAMBINYA

Anita Heiss

DR ANITA HEISS AM is an internationally published, award-winning author of twenty-three books. She is a proud member of the Wiradyuri Nation of central New South Wales, an Ambassador for the Indigenous Literacy Foundation and a Professor of Communications at the University of Queensland. Anita's novel *Bila Yarrudhanggalangdhuray* won the 2022 New South Wales Premier's Literary Awards Indigenous Writers' Prize and was shortlisted for the 2021 ARA Historical Novel Prize. Her latest children's book is *Bidhi Galing (Big Rain)*.

In January 2018, I sat in a hotel room in Wagga Wagga (the place of dance and celebrations) in the giiny (heart) of Wiradyuri ngurambang (Country). It was a Saturday night in summer, and I was full of self-doubt and feelings of inadequacy. I was fifty years old, the author of sixteen books and so many other words, a commentator, a professional speaker, a runner of marathons. But no amount of academic achievement, creative output or life in community had prepared me for learning my Wiradyuri language. I was the first in my immediate miyagan (family) to do so.

As my head throbbed, I felt my self-esteem disappear as fast as my capacity to learn. The first task to master was having to stop 'thinking' in English – the language I had grown up learning and relied on every day. Then I had to understand that there was a completely different grammar system. I read and re-read the relevant pages in *A New Wiradjuri*

Dictionary, compiled by Dr Stan Grant Senior and Dr John Rudder, but it wasn't sinking in. On the verge of yung (tears) of disappointment and failure, I looked at the many resources lying next to me on my bed and said aloud, 'I am never going to get this.'

I almost wanted to give up, but instead I took some time to reflect on the day I'd spent immersed in culture and language. This was thanks to Uncle Stan Grant and his Wiradyuri protégés – Lloyd Dolan, Letetia Harris and Yarri Lambshead – who collectively pass on knowledge as a means of rebuilding the Wiradyuri nation of central New South Wales. They teach the Graduate Certificate in Wiradjuri Language, Culture and Heritage, which is run at the Charles Sturt University (CSU) in Wagga Wagga. Learning is done both in the classroom and outdoors on ngurambang, where we walk and talk where and how our ancestors did. I had long wanted to learn my language, but it wasn't until I was invited to be a guest speaker in the nation-building subject of the course some years before that I saw the extraordinary impact it was having on those studying and made my own commitment to enrol.

Now, in the summer of early 2018, I had walked through cleansing smoke and been part of a welcoming ceremony that grounded me on my ngurambang. I had reunited with some of my miyagan from Tumut and Brungle. I'd made new mudyi-galang (friends) – both Wiradyuri and non-Indigenous – and I'd heard my language spoken with passion for hours on end. It was a spiritually intense moment in my life and my Budhang (Black) giiny was full. I was so incredibly grateful to be there.

During the day, too, I'd found solace in the fact that I wasn't alone in my experience of self-doubt, of the desire to learn colliding with a fear of failure. Most of us students were on the same journey; most of us had come from mayiny (people) denied the right to speak language, to pass on culture, to learn on our own lands, with and from our own mayiny. Policies and acts of protection and assimilation had always had at their core the disconnection of Aboriginal mayiny from ngurambang, culture, community and identity, and this was often overlaid with a belief – a desire – that we would eventually die out and disappear. Learning language as part of rebuilding our nation made it clear to all that we are still here and building capacity. I drifted off to sleep that night mentally exhausted, but grateful for what had led me to that place.

I woke the next ngarin (morning) hoping for some mental breakthrough that would help me understand how to use particular Wiradyuri suffixes and prefixes. What I had learnt as 'tenses' in verbs – past, present and future actions in English – I had to relearn in Wiradyuri as the degree of expression of the action's qualities: not yet real action, actual or real action, intense action, beyond intense action. And each of these degrees has its own suffix. There seemed to be so much more to know and to learn in Wiradyuri than there ever was in English.

I heard the phrase 'Yiradhu marang!' – the Wiradyuri g'day – the minute I arrived in class. And it came with a sweep of the arm like a wave, as language comes from our body. Starting each morning that way set the tone, expectation and empowerment that would flow through our time together.

And I had my breakthrough that day. It wasn't through those prefixes and suffixes. It wasn't while learning to count: ngumbaay, bula, bula ngumbaay. It was when Letetia Harris explained that knowledge would come to me when the ancestors knew I was ready for it that I accepted this was going to be a long journey. To find an absolute belief and faith in that concept led me to trust in myself. To stop doubting, to stop expecting myself to learn and know everything immediately.

Our language has been alive for tens of thousands of years – catching up with it would take a little time.

Hearing language is empowering. When I acknowledge Country in language and am approached by audiences afterwards – both Wiradyuri and non-Indigenous – it is clear that our language has an emotional impact. It is a strong reminder of our presence, of the richness of our culture and of our nationhood.

As a lifetime ambassador for the Indigenous Literacy Foundation (ILF), I see firsthand the importance of reading and writing in First Languages. The ILF has published over ninety books as part of their Community Literacy Projects, and many of them are in eighteen different languages from the remotest communities in Australia. These books assist some of Australia's most disadvantaged people to become self-determining through literacy. And beautiful picture books, presented bilingually, also allow parents and children to connect through story time in a way that gives children the opportunity to have a relationship with books before they start school.

In 2019 the United Nations' International Year of Indigenous Languages reinvigorated the need to reclaim and maintain languages the world over. It emphasised the importance of respecting and honouring traditional languages and encouraged more Wiradyuri citizens to be part of a growing number of mob learning what our old people were denied. The CSU course does not promote itself – all its enrolments come through word of mouth, and all its graduates become proud non-official ambassadors. That's the impact of respecting what we have been gifted through our learning.

Learning language means reclaiming my sovereignty as a Wiradyuri woman, and the experience of reclaiming this sovereignty through the program has been incredibly powerful. Learning and girlang (speaking) has become part of my role in rebuilding our nation. And by finding faith in the wisdom of my ancestors, and trusting in my teachers, in their methods and their lessons, I also found a greater sense of trust in myself.

Wiradyuri values are about yindyamarra (respect), marrumbang (love), ngumbadal (unity), winhangagigilanha (caring for each other). Our values are about the community, not the individual. When I look at the Wiradyuri word ngumambinya – which means trust for help – it reminds me that I need to trust that others will provide help when I need it, whether I ask for it or not. But that trust has a reciprocal value: when we trust in others, they trust in us. As in the case of Wiradyuri responsibility to community, that means giving back. To speak language, to share language and to live the values enshrined in our language.

When people talk about trust, it's often in terms of their relationships with others – their partners, mudyi-galang, miyagan and colleagues. What's clear to me – through ngumambinya and all the Wiradyuri words that can sing through me now as I'm learning – is that we also need to know how to trust in ourselves.

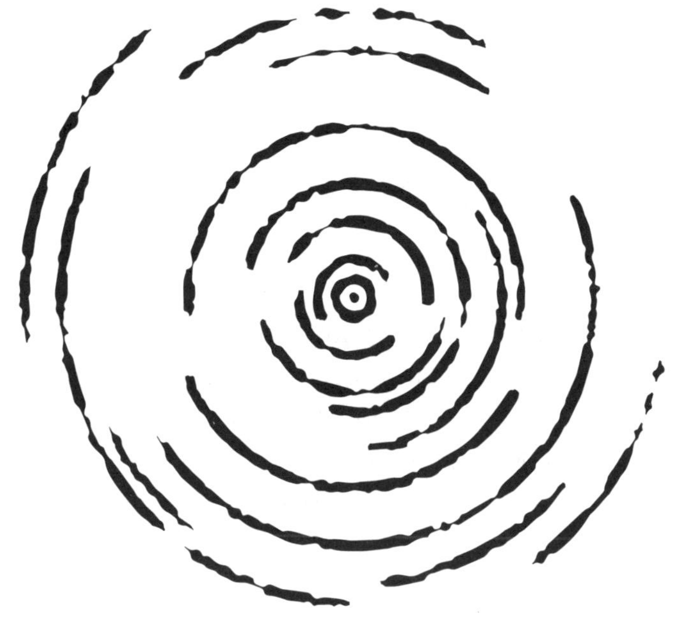

AMAI

Thomas Mayo

THOMAS MAYO is a Kaurareg Aboriginal, Kalkalgal and Erubamle Torres Strait Islander man, who lives on Larrakia Country. He is also the National Indigenous Officer of the Maritime Union of Australia, an author and a lead advocate for the Uluru Statement from the Heart. His website is: thomasmayo.com.au

Amai (pronounced ah-mai) is the Kalaw Lagaw Ya word for cooking in a ground oven using hot stones. Kalaw Lagaw Ya is one of the languages in the Torres Strait Islands.

The Amai way of cooking is an amalgam of who we are as Torres Strait Islanders today. We wrap the meat – mostly turtle, dugong or pork – and usually root vegetables and damper in banana leaves. This is our First Nations culture, embedded and as everlasting as the earth we are born from and will one day return to with our ancestors.

We rub ginger, garlic and soy sauce into the meat for extra flavour. This is the influence of our Asian forefathers, mostly Filipino, Malay and Japanese, who came to the Torres Strait as indentured workers, marrying into our heritage and culture and giving as much as they gained.

We wrap the banana-leaf packages in Alfoil to better hold in the juices and steam – our modern adaptations to survive and thrive today. The Amai is a favourite. For me, it is more than the flavour of the meat – the smoky-leafy, melting-fat meatiness – if heaven on Earth was a flavour this would be it. What really makes the Amai special is the making of the Amai. The memories from when I was a boy. The bond with my father and fellow island men in the hunting, the work, the yarns and laughs as the magic comes together. We love the satisfaction we get from feeding others.

At my mum and dad's place, we always had an Amai hole. Between occasions, the dirt would reclaim the space. And so, in preparation for a cook-up, mostly for special gatherings but sometimes just for joy, Dad and I would carefully dig out the softer dirt that had filled the hole in, pulling out the charred shards of stone that had fractured off the larger stones from the previous cooking, separating them from the still useful, intact stones. We would go for a drive into the bush to find new stones, grey and smooth, usually by a freshwater creek not too far from our home in Darwin.

By then, we would have already been out hunting in my dad's small dinghy. Sometimes just my dad and me. Sometimes with my uncles. Our hunting place is several islands near Darwin with broad flat reefs and fields of seagrass where the turtles and dugong feast.

We also used almond leaves as one of the layers in the making of the Amai. We used to have an almond tree in the backyard. It is gone now. The victim of a cyclone. It was my favourite for climbing. We tend to use gum-tree leaves now – they give the meat a light eucalyptus flavour.

As we marinated pieces of meat, ready for cooking, a big fire would be ablaze in the hole. The stones were placed among the stack of now-burning wood. The fire dies down to coals. The fire's heat now held by the stones.

We use steel rakes, tongs and work-hardened hands to remove as many coals as possible and to place the shiny packages of food and stones for efficient cooking. There is an art to this – an unwritten science. While I make this vital arrangement, I feel an experience of Eldership and the hum of countless generations at play.

The leaves – almond, eucalyptus or whatever plant chosen – are now piled onto the cooking meat. The green leaves provide steam, flavour and protection. Wet hessian bags are laid on top, then a final layer of dirt is shovelled on. Eyes search the warm earthen mound for escaping steam that must be covered with a little more dirt.

For a time, calculated only by experience and good sense, unexplainable in a cookbook, the magic happens under camouflage. If the Amai is for a feast after a ceremonial gathering, we cook large saucepans of other favourite foods as we wait.

We are sweaty and hot, smiling and playfully mocking, reminiscing in good company. Usually enjoying a cold beer and some barbecued offal from the turtle or dugong, dipped in chillies, vinegar and belachan.

One of the old men takes a shovel. The young men and boys watch, and quickly move to assist. To take instruction. To learn. The dirt is carefully scraped off the hessian cloth. The hessian bags are peeled away, one by one, exposing the browned, still-steamy leaves. Dripping packages of gloriously flavoursome food are lifted from the earth for slicing, sampling – a cook's privilege – and serving in a traditional island spread.

As an islander born and raised so far from my island homes, the Amai is island life on the mainland. It means cooking in the ground using hot stones. It is the aroma of earth and steam and damp, hot leaves and glorious juicy food.

Amai is language, culture and the bonds among island men, and the satisfaction we get from feeding our families. It is love between fathers and sons.

GIBAM GARANDALEHN

Ellen van Neerven

ELLEN VAN NEERVEN is an award-winning writer of Mununjali Yugambeh and Dutch heritage. Ellen has authored two poetry collections, *Comfort Food* and *Throat*, one work of fiction, *Heat and Light*, and a non-fiction title, *Personal Score: Sport, Culture, Identity.*

*

Giba garandalehn
Minyanggu giribawahla nganyi
Minyanggilehla ngaya mubu, ngi?

*

Bahbuny
Ngawragi wanyi gulgunu ngalingah
Nga giyagi 'Gumerahla wanyi ngay'

*

Guwany
Minyanggu giribawahla nganyi
Yawun nyanggai'jahra wahlugaya, ngi?

★

Gurumgan guwalehn
Gannganah bangehn wahlu

★

Gamay yarga
Minyanggu giribawahla nganyi
Nyumbahla nganyi nguy yugam dagarah ngay, ngi?

★

Ganggah jimi
Yugam nuwangbil
Barehbanan'galehla yarabilnu

★

Dalgah
Jagunu
Yarabih barehbanu

★

full moon –
why you keep me awake
what do you have in store for me tomorrow?

*

Nana
I wanted to speak to you in our language
and tell you I love you

*

brush-tail possum –
why you keep me awake
is the night like day to you?

*

stars broke
when they heard you died
dust fell at our feet

*

strong wind –
why you keep me awake
is it to teach me I am not alone?

★

take the feather
over the bird
dream in song

★

make music
from the land
sing in dreams

Yugambeh interpretations were provided by Shaun Davis (Yugambeh Library).

MUNATHIYA

Adam Thompson

ADAM THOMPSON is a pakana writer from lutruwita (Tasmania). He is the author of *Born Into This* and *Little J and Big Cuz: The Stormy Night*, and his work has appeared in several anthologies and literary journals. Adam also writes and produces for screen and is co-director of Kutikina Productions – the first-ever pakana screen production company.

As a kid I thought
pataway was munathiya
wangata through
concrete veins.
Its essence drawn from earth
burned, ground and leached
into smoke-puff clouds
and a shit-stained sea
by the paper mill lining the highway
remnant of another time
built by curious men in overalls
with twisted moustaches, monocles
and top hats on the weekends.
I'd look on from the car
with my comic stack
and spine-battered hardcovers
of minstrels, treasure
that old-school library smell

and I'd wonder
who is to blame for all this?

Now, I gaze out of the restaurant
from the hills behind my home
and see it is munathiya.
wangata through
ploughed earth
churned up and divided
into barren rectangles
with a treeless horizon
by the farmers on their tractors
wearing red caps and flannies
hidden wives, their kid's skid-marks
blemish straight dairy roads
with annoying ninety-degree turns.
I look down at my taste-plate
the smoked salmon, lettuce
Tasmanian cheese
stomach growling
and I finish my wine, thinking
how can they keep ruining the land?

The minungkana find the trees
with needy claws.
Their pungkatina is munathiya.
They crack gumnuts and cry
in the still afternoon.

It's always still when they arrive
but not when they leave
finding a twisted bough
gumnuts fall
like rain
like dust
like stones
among the saplings.
And I watch through my windshield
as they flee from the car
with its dual exhaust
a beautiful note.
They are gone now
from people, from sight
and I question
why are they so rare these days?

My Country is munathiya.
wangata through
a corrupt government
in bed with industry.
It's them
always them
dashing our world
as ochre on rock
as sea on sand
into pulp-like mass
eyes shielded

bearing no responsibility
turning away
from accountability
while we can only watch
and wonder
how can they fucking live with themselves?

My Country is munathiya
now so am I
and I wangata through
very real veins.
And there is nobody to blame, but me.

BUWALWOEYDHAY

Jimi Bani

JIMI BANI is a Wagadagam man from Mabuyag Island in the Torres Strait. Jimi has worked with most Australian theatre companies and performed internationally at London's Barbican Centre. Jimi has six acting nominations to his name, including a National Dreamtime Award for Best Male Actor in 2017, a Silver Logie for Most Outstanding Actor in a Television Drama (*Mabo*) and an AACTA Award for Best Lead Actor in a Television Drama (*Mabo*) in 2012, among others.

Hi, my name is Jimi Bani. I'm a Wagadagam and Peudu man from Zenadth Kes (Torres Strait). My bloodline also runs to the Butchulla Nation, Kaurareg Nation, and Rotuma and Solomon Islands. I was born and bred on Waibene (Thursday Island) on the lands of the Kaurareg Nation, Zenadth Kes.

My language word I've chosen is Buwalwoeydhay. This word comes from the language called Kalaw Lagaw Ya, which originated from the western part of Zenadth Kes. Buwalwoeydhay (boowul-were-y-thai) means the growth of the vegetable Buwa (bua) or 'wild yam' and Woeydhay means 'cutting or peeling off'. So it is the actual development, growth, maturing, cleaning and preparation process of the vegetable.

Wild yam is produced underground like potatoes. The beginning stages of the development of the vegetable starts off looking like an onion, then the formation grows into the look of a cabbage, then the look of a hairy sprout. When the mound protrudes with cracks and hairs through the soil, you know it is ready to be dug out. Then it is cleaned by peeling the hairy skin off and this process of peeling is called Buwalwoeydhay.

Why did I choose this word over the many amazing words and phrases that Kalaw Lagaw Ya has to offer? Well, in our cultural lore and practices, Buwalwoeydhay is also the Initiation process of a young boy or girl transitioning into adulthood. There is a stage when our young boys (I can only speak on the boy side), in the teenager period, may have a communication breakdown with their parents or guardians. In our society today we say, 'Oh it's okay, that's what happens, they're teenagers now,' or, 'It's expected, so be ready for it.' But in our cultural lore and practices, that is a sign it is time for the young boy to be taken away by his Wadhuwam (maternal uncles) from his parents or guardians and go through men's business, Buwalwoeydhay.

During this process, the young fella will learn how to survive, how to provide, how to be a warrior. The uncles will teach him and share everything to the best of their knowledges and experiences. The boy will get detailed teachings on: making his own hunting tools and preparing them; understanding the weather of the land, sea, wind and constellations; how to hunt and to provide families with shares from a catch; how to cook; how to make traditional ceremonial tools and perform with them. How to drive cars, open up a bank account; how to pay bills, follow his dreams and again survive.

Amazing things happen during this time. Along with all the blessings of wealth and knowledge being handed down, there are two important things that happen. One, the young boy will get to know who he is, his strengths and weaknesses, his roles and responsibilities in our community, his purpose and his belonging. And two, through the conversations with his uncles, he will get to know who his parents or guardians are. Now this is very important. See, from the boy's knowledge and perspective, he only knows them from what he experiences in the first sixteen or seventeen years of his life. But stories will be given to him about who his parents were and the sacrifices that they made to make sure he has a roof over his head, food to eat, water to drink, clothes on his back, or to go on an expensive school trip, even though they're poor. These are just some examples of their sacrifices. From this information, he will appreciate and respect his parents or guardians even more. He will understand the meaning of the words: value, responsibility and accountability.

After this happens, his Wadhuwam will let the parents or guardians know that he is ready to go back home. Then there will be a ceremony, where the Wadhuwam will present the boy to the parents or guardians as a man. He went as a boy and came back as a man. His appreciation towards them will be evident. Their communication will lift to another level of conversation, and he will have more presence in the household or community to help carry any heavy lifting and make it lighter.

This process can take years, but it is up to the Wadhuwam to see when the boy is ready. When practising it proper, the young fella will be empowered, and that's what that lore is designed for. This structure is in many cultures here in Australia and around the world.

This piece was written in consultation with Wagadagam Tribal Elder, Cultural Advisor Councillor and Bani Consultant Gabriel Bani.

TJUKURRPA

Elizabeth Ellis

DR ELIZABETH ELLIS is a Senior Ngaanyatjarra lore woman, artist, writer, educator, researcher and linguist from the Ngaanyatjarra Lands of the Gibson Desert in Western Australia. She has committed her life to supporting and facilitating communication between her Ngaanyatjarra people, who were the last Indigenous tribe uncontacted by Western culture in Australia, and the non-Indigenous people in our Australian community.

Hello, my Aboriginal names are Marrkilyi Warnngupayi (Elizabeth Ellis). I am a Senior Ngaatjatjarra/Ngaanyatjarra woman from the Aboriginal community of Warakurna in Western Australia. My parents and grandparents explained to us that the word Tjukurrpa means everything in our world. Tjukurrpa is miirl-miirlpa (sacred).

A very long time ago, our world and we as Ngaanyatjarra and Western Desert people, as well as other Aboriginal people in Australia, and even internationally, came into being. The ancestral beings created our world. We called this the Tjukurrpa time – the creation time – commonly known in Australia as the Dreaming. The ancestral beings created everything in our world: land, water, plants, food, people, and even our languages and much more. This is how we perceive Tjukurrpa. This time has no equivalent in the European culture. Our word Tjukurrpa has many other meanings as well, such as: the natural features within our environment associated with our creation story; news, story or message; dream; birthmark or totem.

Indigenous and non-Indigenous people have attempted to explain the meaning of our special word Tjukurrpa. Many anthropologists have tried to define the meaning of Tjukurrpa and some have done a great job, but others have done a terrible job.

I quote anthropologist Fred Myers's explanation of the word Tjukurrpa:

> Because the Tjukurrpa touches on so many dimensions of Western Desert people's lives, it possesses no single or infinite existence. Instead, it represents a projection into the symbolic spaces of various social processes, hence the social meanings of the Tjukurrpa only become apparent in the penetration into every aspect of Aboriginal life, by providing a guide to all social order, social activity, and communication.

I will give you a few examples of how Tjukurrpa is part of everyday life. Wanarn is one of the communities in the Ngaanyatjarra lands where I come from and is commonly known as the Seven Sisters Community because the Seven Sisters travelled through and spent time there, therefore creating the environment that is there to this day. The Seven Sisters songlines is a very important and high-order Tjukurrpa, and that Tjukurrpa lives not only in the past – it continues in the present and into the future, because we the people make it live by telling the stories, retelling the stories and singing the songs, continually singing the songs and dancing the dances.

Wanarn waterhole was created by the Seven Sisters and the pile of rocks next to the waterhole are the sisters. Yurla, the man chasing them, is there too, as a rock, just to the south. The Seven Sisters are there as the big rock and the waterhole. The young children of that community tell many stories about the Seven Sisters in the classroom. Some of the funny things that they've said or come up with are stories like 'the Seven Sisters, they never had a television', but then sometimes a child would draw a picture and I've seen a drawing of the Seven Sisters sitting in a cave watching television.

We also say hello to the gum-tree that is Yurla, on the side of the road, and we call him Tjamu (grandfather). 'Hello, Tjamu.' There's also another gum-tree closer to Warakurna that is Yurla. Near Warakurna we asked Yurla to bless us with a successful hunting trip. Young men from other Ngaanyatjarra lands are fearful of going to Wanarn because the Seven Sisters are in an agitated state due to being chased by Yurla, and they may accidentally harm the young men.

NGINHA-GULIA NYIANG

Jeanine Leane

JEANINE LEANE is a Wiradjuri writer, poet and academic from south-west New South Wales. Her poetry, short stories, critique and essays have been published in *Hecate: An Interdisciplinary Journal of Women's Liberation*, *Australian Poetry Journal*, *Antipodes*, *Overland* and *Sydney Review of Books.* Jeanine has published widely in the area of Aboriginal literature, writing otherness, literary critique and creative non-fiction. *Gawimarra: Gathering* is her most recent poetry collection.

These words cry out and I hear them – learn to mould
and shape them like clay.
There should have been a time for such words
for this word – 'Nginha Nyiang'
and a word for such time 'Guwayu'.

How clunky these are as I first stumble over them.
Grappling like the child I should have been when I first
felt them – 'Winungah Dilinyi', sang them – 'Babiyi',
spoke them – 'Yayi'.

Now my clumsy tongue struggles over each new
syllable my Country 'Ngurambang' gives me.

Each one I want to devour like the sweetest thing
'Wiluray Bang Gula-dhayi' I ever tasted.
I want to suck every shred of the marrow
'Dundumbirra' from each solid sound.

I want to swallow it whole 'Darra-Marra'
to know what it is to eat for the first time.
I want to feel like the child born to these words
'Gudha Dhurrinya Nginha Nyiang'.

Wiradjuri interpretations were provided by Aunty Elaine Lomas.

BARKA

Paul Collis

PAUL COLLIS is a Barkindji man, born in Bourke in far-western New South Wales on the Darling River. Paul has a Bachelor of Arts and a Doctorate in Communications. He lives in Canberra and works as a creative writing academic at the University of Canberra. *Dancing Home* was his first novel and won the 2016 David Unaipon Award and the 2018 ACT Book of the Year Award. Paul's first book of poetry is *Nightmares Run Like Mercury.*

I come from Bourke, which is about six … seven hundred kilometres from Canberra. Up near the Queensland–South Australia border, on the river Darling. And the Darling River was named after Sir Ralph Darling. But it had another name – it still has that name. And more and more Barkindji people are starting to call the river by its original name, and that's the word I want to share today.

We call that river barka and we're Barkindji people. It's a derivative of barka. Barka roughly translated into English means 'my darling'. I wonder what them old fellas would have thought when they said, 'What's that you say, what's that word?' 'The Darling River.' 'Hmmm, which way?' I hope they smiled when they found out that they were calling the river what it means.

In Bill Gammage's great book *The Biggest Estate on Earth* – if you haven't read it, get it, it's an extraordinary piece of work – he says that upon contact with Aboriginal people whitefellas found the country in pristine condition. Water flowed, animals were able to move freely between places and people, nothing was hindered and the word that whitefellas used mainly to describe Australia in those early settlement days was park. They said the land was so well managed that you could drive a carriage through the bush as you would in Hyde Park in London. So next time you go for a drive, look at all that rubbish scrub that's not been tended to and think about that word barka, 'my darling'.

I don't know much Barkindji language. When I was small, my grandfather could speak eight languages. My nan could speak the same number of languages. Nan was a Kunya woman from Queensland. Grandfather was a Barkindji man from Gundabooka, near Louth. I said to Mum before she died, 'How come they could talk to each other?' and she said, 'Oh, there's this other language, there's some crossover words.' And language is like that – it's more than a communication tool, it's more than something to name or possess. It's something else.

We think the Darling River was made by the rainbow serpent because it rained – the rainbow serpent is a snake – it's woman's Dreaming, it's woman's Country. We come through female lines – through matriarchy – so those women carried our history, our laws. They held the Country. Very different way of operating.

I asked my grandfather, 'What am I?' and he said, 'You're Barkindji boy, like me.' 'Okay … how do I do that?' And when I was eleven, I asked him, 'Grandfather, why don't you teach me Barkindji language?' He said, 'Who would you talk to when I go?' He felt that the language would die out, would not be useful. He didn't understand. I don't think he understood how speaking in language can produce different ways of thinking and meaning. Many of the great struggles Aboriginal people face today are modern problems. I can't find a word in the traditional languages that I've looked at for cancer, for example. Did we have cancer before whitefellas got here? That's a real serious question. It's just assumed that we did, like other people. But maybe we didn't. I don't know.

Badger Bates is my Senior Elder. Badger's from Wilcannia, about 500 kilometres south of Bourke. If you haven't been to Wilcannia, it's an experience. A lot of whitefellas that go out there and teach, they love the people and that area, but when they come back and I say, 'Where you been?' and they say, 'We'll tell ya ... Bit rough, nice Country though. And the Darling River ... We have never known it not to run.'

I ask you this: 'What is a river? What happens if there's no water in it – is it still a river?' I did some research looking at how Barkindji people managed the river before whitefellas got here. Two of the women, my cousins, older than me, said, 'Make sure you tell that Paul to come up here.' They had a story about this thing:

'I'll tell you about this, boy.'

'Oh yeah, what?'

'I'll tell you about woodagunna.'

'Woodagunna, what's that?'

'It's this big thing in the water … waterspout …'

Those women been holding that story for thirty years. They were on every management plan over the last thirty-five years to try to protect the river. You might have seen the *7.30* report about breaking the pump meters so they can store water, take water out of the river. The river is almost dry, it has been dry in Bourke for a couple years. It's almost dry, but out there is a flood plain – real flat – that goes for hundreds of kilometres either side of the river. When it rains, water goes back into the system. You can't get in there now because of farms. Badger says that we know that crime rates go up in Aboriginal communities along the river bank when the water level drops down – those kids aren't out there participating in culture, they're in town.

YURNARNGU

Charmaine Papertalk Green

CHARMAINE PAPERTALK GREEN was born in Eradu, Western Australia, and is a proud Wajarri, Badimaya and Wilunyu woman of the Yamaji Nation. A visual artist, author, poet and storyteller, she shares her cultural knowledge in many different spheres. Charmaine has written five books, won several awards including the prestigious Australian Literature Society Gold Medal, and her poetry is studied as part of the primary school curriculum. She has been involved with the Yamaji Art Centre in Geraldton for over twenty-two years, and she is currently their chairperson.

There are so many evocative objects, catchcries, terms and favourite Yamaji phrases that offer a memory bridge to one's childhood, family, Country, cultural practices and culture. I love so many Yamaji words and phrases that bring sense and meaning to our reality. I spent a little time reflecting on one Yamaji word or term that remains in the pocket close to my heart, one I think of many times while navigating this complex life. It comes from my maternal grandmother's cultural group, Wajarri, and has travelled with me on my life road. The word is Yurnarngu, which in Wajarri means 'really good; great; terrific; very good; bloody good'.

I recall in my childhood and as a teenager growing up in Mullewa using Yurnarngu often with other Yamaji cultural members to describe someone doing something we thought was really good or better than good. When we offered Yurnarngu to someone it was always accompanied by a hand/arm signal, and the way we said it – the length and pitch – was in sync with the verbal message. We weren't ashamed to give praise and let someone know that we appreciated what they had done or were doing was above just 'good'. The word and the hand/arm signal are a positive Yamaji message moving together, and this is why I cherish the term Yurnarngu.

I chose this term because it belongs within the Yamaji way of being and is an everyday Yamaji cultural practice not heard or seen very often anymore when it should be, because we live in a reality where Yamaji people are repeatedly seen in a negative way. And everything positive and good about Yamaji culture and people needs to outweigh any damaging or harmful views imposed on the cultural interface. I love the way the word Yurnarngu sounds, is pronounced, and belongs with a hand/arm signal sweeping through the air so the intended receiver can see the message even if they can't hear it. A similar message communicated in English, for example when saying 'excellent; brilliant; very good; good on you' and so forth, feels so far removed from the Yamaji space and doesn't have the same impact.

Our Yamaji Excellence can be pushed behind, pushed down or not even celebrated by the Yamaji community in a Yamaji way, and I personally don't like that. I say this because words and terms like Yurnarngu were handed down from our old people for our use and these words appear to be slowly disappearing down the generations as more Yamaji are trodden into the town way of life. The town way of life, or colonial spaces, where the Western way of life is imposed and Yamaji culture is not valued as part of the system, are spheres where culture and cultural knowledge clash, and these tensions are a challenge to navigate.

I want to briefly explain why I say the use of the Wajarri word Yurnarngu is gradually declining. When I was sixteen years old, I left my hometown Mullewa for schooling, and after twenty years I returned home to live on Country in Geraldton on the coast, one hundred kilometres from Mullewa. When I returned to Yamaji Country, I noticed a significant language shift, especially among the younger generations. The Wajarri word Barndi was used extensively and I couldn't hear Yurnarngu. Barndi means 'good; okay; sweet; clever; easy; well; pretty'. The other terms I heard the younger people use quite frequently were 'deadly; solid; neat; dardy; wicked' and sometimes a Noongar word Moorditj, but I didn't hear Yurnarngu. I had heard all these words before and had used them, but the term dardy was unfamiliar. This term I am told is from the south-west of Western Australia. I wondered why people were not using Yurnarngu? Was it just a Mullewa thing or a Wajarri thing or both?

Over the years I have heard Yurnarngu said by a few Yamaji people down at the beach, at a concert or in Mullewa. Other than that, when wanting to use a Yamaji term to describe something good most people use the Wajarri word Barndi or Aboriginal English terms like dardy, which doesn't sound very Aboriginal or Yamaji to me at all. In reality the shifting sands of words and Yamaji language in Geraldton and Mullewa has been harsh, and there are many reasons for this. These reasons are varied, complex and multilayered, with connections to the impact of colonisation through the *Aborigines Act 1905 (WA)*, the government's assimilation policy and the displacement of Yamaji from their traditional lands. The violence against language speakers and Yamaji languages contributed to many Yamaji words and phrases being replaced with English and Aboriginal English. All of these factors forcing language shifts makes the fight to keep the term Yurnarngu alive in Yamaji minds that more important. There is nothing wrong with striving and praising beyond Barndi (good) to Yurnarngu (beyond excellent) – we need not shy away from giving or receiving praise and positive messages in a society that can be highly critical.

I knew all was not lost in this language shift when I received a congratulatory email in 2023 from a younger Wajarri woman using the term Yurnarngu to send me an encouraging and supportive message rather than any of the other terms or words mentioned here. Yurnarngu is our Yamaji word for Blak Excellence.

GED

Terri Janke

DR TERRI JANKE is a Meriam and Wuthathi woman and an international authority on Indigenous Cultural and Intellectual Property (ICIP). She is the owner and Managing Director of Terri Janke and Company, an award-winning legal and consulting firm founded in 2000. The firm has a vision to empower Indigenous peoples to manage their culture, attain their business goals and to assert their ICIP. The protocols in her book *True Tracks: Respecting Indigenous knowledge and culture* are used widely to support collaboration with Indigenous and non-Indigenous peoples. Terri was a co-chief author of the 2021 *State of the Environment* report.

Ged means home. People are Ged. Land is Ged. Ged is a Meriam Mir language word, from the Torres Strait, the islands between Cape York and Papua New Guinea. Meriam Mir comes from Mer, or Murray Island. Ged is island. Ged is a word I have heard Meriam people speak. It's in the names of organisations – being strengthened through community use.

It's a simple word, but its meaning is holistic. Ged means Country, referring to the land, and like the word Country, it also means connection, belonging, home. Because the land is home, and home is the land. The land is our lore, custom and knowledge. It's our language, our ancestry, our spirit. We call the land Country to refer to the relationship between all these elements. Country is our culture. It is a universal law for Indigenous cultures that you look after the land, because the land will look after you.

Caring for Country is a reciprocal relationship and the land and seas, the animals, fish and plants become sick if not managed by its people, and in turn, its people will become unwell too. Healthy Country means healthy people. First Nations people have lived according to this understanding as the role of custodians of Country is embedded in our way of life. First Nations people look after Country like it is kin.

Ged is connection to the environment. Through a longstanding relationship and lived experience within the land and waters, Indigenous peoples derived knowledge and cultural systems that have been passed down for countless generations. They developed a holistic and unparalleled knowledge about the environment – an understanding of the unique ebbs and flows of the natural world – from which they weaved their culture. This cultural art, craft and traditional knowledge is passed down from generation to generation through story, dance, song and language.

Land management practices are embedded in Indigenous culture. These practices have been tested, learnt, used, adapted and passed down to the next generation. They sustained Indigenous societies for thousands of years, for they are knowledge systems whose foundations lie in sustainability, ensuring the land is strong for this generation and generations to come.

Indigenous fire management, known as cultural burning, was used to protect cultural sites, to clear access for paths on Country, for hunting, for agricultural purposes and for ceremony. Cultural burning keeps the land healthy and helps to prevent catastrophic bushfire outbreaks. Since the loss of ability to care for Country, we have seen the environment decline in health. Without being able to access the land and make decisions about Country, Indigenous peoples are unable to practise their culture – a web of systems of stewardship.

There is much we can take by way of land management traditions to care for Country and keep Ged strong. To maintain the strength of First Nations cultures is to maintain the traditional knowledge, practices and customs that nurture the environment.

Ged is family. I am a daughter, sister, niece, wife, mother and aunty. Ged is ancestors. I have two grandmothers who were born in the Torres Strait. I am connected to Meriam people through my paternal great-grandmother, Azey Leha, the mother of my grandmother, Agnes Blanco. Agnes was born on Mer in 1921 in the village of Gigrid, of the Peibre clan. She was the daughter of Azey Leha, a Meriam woman, and Victor Blanco. Victor's mother, Annie, who married Juan Blanco from the Phillipines, was from Old Mapoon in Cape York. Grandma Agnes attended Sacred Heart Convent on Thursday Island before moving to the mainland during the Second World War.

I only met Agnes once, when she reunited with my father. It was in Mossman in Far North Queensland on the mainland, not far from Cairns, where we grew up as kids. My grandmother died two years after we met. I remember her hair, her face, her hands. I remember looking at her feet when she held out her hand to meet me.

I grew up on the mainland of Australia in Cairns, Canberra and then Sydney. I am sad that I did not grow up speaking Meriam Mir language. The disconnection of family and heritage for First Nations people has been devastating on language practice. Like many Aboriginal and Torres Strait Islander people, my ancestors were forced to speak a foreign language. The loss of people and the removal of children silenced the words spoken on Country. Aboriginal and Torres Strait Islander languages were spoken on lands for tens of thousands of years before colonisation, and Australia's first languages are considered endangered.

Today there are many Indigenous groups revitalising languages and making them strong again. Their work includes recording language, and examining old records in archives, notes and books written by researchers and linguists. This is where my work in Indigenous cultural and intellectual property (ICIP) comes in to help. It aims to empower Indigenous people to understand their rights to their culture, language and stories, and helps non-Indigenous people understand how to engage with ICIP respectfully. My work hopes to prevent Indigenous people from being disconnected from their inherent cultural heritage again.

The marked decline of those speaking Meriam Mir as an everyday language has had an immense impact, and it is good to see the strong Meriam Elders speaking language and revitalising it as a community. I am grateful to speakers who revitalise and share language and culture today. One such person is Meriam linguist Uncle Benny Mabo, who helped me put together words for the 2021 *State of the Environment* chapter on Indigenous themes, a report of which I was co-chief author. Uncle Benny Mabo has since passed away, but he generously helped me with translation. I was writing about Indigenous ways of knowing and seeing, and caring for the environmental challenges of today and the future. As the world's oldest living culture, Indigenous people have dealt with environmental change since time immemorial, but this chapter was to be the first time that Indigenous voices would be heard in this report.

I wrote down some words in English like poetry and Uncle Benny Mabo translated the words into Meriam Mir. I wanted the language words to describe land and Country. I wanted to describe that the years of living on land and waters, and interacting with it, and celebrating and respecting it, keeps Indigenous people strong, and in turn keeps Country strong. We care for Country, and it cares for us. Culture is home, culture is Ged. This is what we came up with:

> 'Uteb Azimwaretli.' Protect our land.
> 'Keriba au Tonaride Keriba Ged Kelar Aiswerli.'
> The strength of our culture gives strength to our land.

PRESERVING NGUNNAWAL LANGUAGE THROUGH MEDIA

Dan Bourchier

DAN BOURCHIER has been an agent of change in the media, proudly representing his Indigenous heritage and the LGBTQIA+ community. He grew up in the outback Northern Territory mining town of Tennant Creek. Dan is the host of *Mornings* and *Weekends* on the ABC News Channel and is the Chair of the ABC's Bonner Committee. In 2023 he was the ABC's Voice/Referendum Correspondent. Dan regularly hosts and appears on major national ABC programs and events, including *The Drum*, *Four Corners* and *Insiders*, and reports across radio, televsion, online and social media.

The very first acknowledgement of First Nations people on the ABC network was done through respectful, culturally safe, lengthy discussions with the Ngunnawal Elders of Canberra. This resulted in their voices being heard and celebrated on ABC programs, as well as the groundbreaking use of traditional languages and place names being shared, which has spread further afield in Australian media.

'Language is universal and it should be shared,' Senior Ngunnawal Elder of Canberra Aunty Ros Brown told me. This powerful statement shows both the vision of Elders to see the importance of First Nations language, and the generosity in sharing it and inviting all Australians to be part of that conversation.

Aunty Ros is respected in the community we both live in, where her connections link back thousands of years, while mine are as a visitor to her Country, on and off, for the last decade. I first got to know her when

I became the newsreader of ABC Canberra's flagship 7:00 pm *News* in 2017. One of my first priorities at that time was to get to know the Elders, yarn with them about their Country, and talk to them about my story and who I am.

The more I sat with and listened to the Elders, the greater my depth of understanding grew of their connection and ties to the Country beneath our feet – to the places that were sacred and central to their stories – and how in turn those stories offered understanding and context to those connections. And language – like dance, song and storytelling – is a tool used to preserve and pass on those stories.

'Language is important to the very essence of humanity, it's how we communicate,' Aunty Ros said. 'We were blessed with being given speech so we can talk to each other. It connects people. You create beautiful songs out of language, and tell your stories through the songs. Language is everything.'

But Ngunnawal, like many of the First Nations languages spoken across Australia for tens of thousands of years, has been eroded by time, and by government policies that sought to disconnect speakers from their Country and shared identity.

As a journalist, I see every day how the words we use give context and meaning to the world around us – and help to make sense of our place within it. I see the importance of language in how we seek to be understood and to understand others and where they are coming from.

It's also a reminder of what has been lost to my family. I don't know the language of my ancestors – so much has been removed as a result of deliberate policies aimed at doing just that. I do know they had their names changed and were forbidden from speaking in their own tongue. I also know how language was used against my family in the form of taunts thrown at my late great-aunty Rita, forcing her into a toilet cubicle, where she would eat lunch alone rather than experience schoolyard racism. She faced language as a weapon.

Language and its power has underpinned my career, and has driven me to storytelling and helping others to tell their stories. It's why I thought the suggestion from my colleague Senior Editor Jan Pritchard to introduce First Nations language on the ABC in Canberra was so important. But before that, hearing from those Elders, and listening deeply to their experiences with the media, was crucial. In a sense, it was like a mini version of truth-telling. The team and I listened to understand.

I remember sitting at the news desk that night, in October 2019, with Elders in the studio. Ngunnawal was written on the screen behind me, and for the first time, I spoke their language on television – 'Yuma' for hello and 'Yarra' for goodbye. I remember feeling underwhelmed, wondering if all our work was simply symbolic, without an impact. But the Elders there that night felt the opposite.

The late Senior Ngunnawal Elder Aunty Agnes OAM said at the time of the first acknowledgement on air that it was like a 'huge boulder being pushed into the water, we don't know what ripple effects it will have'. Another Ngunnawal Elder, Dr Aunty Caroline Hughes AM, who voiced her language on the radio, said that for her it was a sign of 'coming full circle'.

'Growing up we could never share our language with non-Indigenous people. Language was to be kept secret to keep us safe,' she said. 'I was so scared to speak my language as a child – scared I'd be taken away. If I said something and was asked about it, I'd quickly change it, for fear of what might happen. It's like we were made to be ashamed of being Aboriginal.'

Over time, I would come to see the 'ripple effect' the Elders spoke of and, of course, their wisdom about the substantive impact of symbolic change. 'I've had so many non-Indigenous people coming up to me, recognising my voice, and wanting to have a conversation about the language, and about my people,' Aunty Caroline said. 'Everyone that approaches me speaks so highly of it – and other Indigenous people are so proud.'

It led to a renewed local interest in Ngunnawal language. It also initiated similar processes to embed language and recognition across the ABC. Even further, some at the ABC have helped other organisations and companies to kick off their own processes to acknowledge and recognise First Nations people.

Aunty Ros captured the power of language more eloquently than I ever could. 'Using language gives you a sense of belonging,' Aunty told me.

BARAYGIR

Daniel Browning

DANIEL BROWNING is an Aboriginal journalist, broadcaster, documentary maker, sound artist and writer. He is the ABC's Editor of Indigenous Radio, overseeing the longstanding programs *Speaking Out* and *Awaye!* He also presents *The Art Show* on ABC Radio National. His book *Close to the Subject: Selected works* includes critical essays on Indigenous art, his journalism and memoir. Daniel is from the Bundjalung people of far-northern New South Wales on his father's side, while his maternal ancestors are the Kullilli people of south-western Queensland and the Yugambeh-speaking people of the Gold Coast hinterland.

I come from Saltwater Country on the far-north coast of New South Wales where Bundjalung is spoken. And I must thank the writer Evelyn Araluen, who shared this word with me in a poem she wrote about learning Bundjalung on Dharawal Country.

It's a word that has dual meanings, but it also expresses the way we speak in metaphor. We find relationships between things, between people and the natural world. We are just part of an ecology of living things, who exist in relationship to each other.

The word then is baraygir. It means the youngest child. But it also means the top of the trees or the tip of something – the apex, the highest or terminal point. Upwards, above.

Baray is a noun, an adjective and an adverb. It can even mean 'God', literally 'up at'. So in one word, Bundjalung defines a relationship to another human being, as well as the tip of a mountain. It's a social and familial term, as well as a spatial term, and it neatly brings the human and the natural world into correlation. That's the power of language, and of subjectivity – it describes the world as we see it, as an ecology of things in which human beings are just a part.

I'd like to quickly share another – it's the Bundjalung word for nephew, but explicitly for a man's sister's son. So, the sons of my sister. The word is burudjam. My nephew Bodhi is eighteen months old, and you should see his face light up when I call him that. He loves to hear the roll of the 'r'. This beautiful child is both baraygir, the youngest, and burudjam, the son of my sister.

I come from Booninybah, the place of the echidna. Booning is echidna. Nearby is a lake called Wommin, which means to grow fat – it's a site of abundance where my ancestors left bush game to thrive, so they could hunt it when they didn't want to eat ukre or pipis and shellfish. Across the water is Ukerebagh, place of the ukre.

The word for white man is dagay. It also means 'ghost' or 'corpse'. The word for boundary rider or drover is dagayu or dagayiyu, literally 'travelling white man', when they came searching for land to graze their livestock on. Dagayu or dagayiyu (jug-igh-ee-ooh) was corrupted into the Australian English term jackeroo.

There's a subjectivity in these words that you can't deny. They express so much about my ancestors, about the way they saw the world and how they positioned themselves in it.

It is their gift to us.

KOOROONDEE

Vicki Couzens

VICKI COUZENS is a Gunditjmara woman from the western districts of Victoria. Vicki acknowledges her Ancestors and Elders who guide her work. She has worked in Aboriginal community affairs for forty-five years. Vicki's contributions in the reclamation, regeneration and revitalisation of cultural knowledge and practice extend across the arts and creative cultural expression spectrum including language revitalisation, ceremony, community arts, public art, visual and performing arts, and writing. She is a Senior Knowledge Custodian for Possum Skin Cloak Story and Language Reclamation and Revival in her Keerray Woorroong Mother Tongue.

Kooroondee poondeeya-yee kandeeyt, wanga
Behave properly, live in proper relationship, listen, understand

Wangangootyoong wooka ba mana wangangootyoong,
poondeeya-yee tyamateeyt
Respect, give and hold/receive respect, live in Law

Matoowee-matoowee-keel matooweematoowee keeyn
meerreeng-ee
Have kindness/compassion, be kind care/love for Country

Keeyn Kayampaa-yt-ee
Care/love for all Kin

Leerpeen meerreeng-ee, karweeyn meerreeng-ee
Sing to Country Dance to Country

Laka-wanoong ngeerang wooroong-ngeeye, leerpeen-
wanoong ngeerang wooroong-ngeeye
We speak our Mother Tongue, we sing our Mother Tongue

Karweeyn-wanoong ngeerang wooroong-ngeeye,
keeyn toopoo-wanoong meerreeng-ngeeye
We dance our ngeerang wooroong-ngeeye, we love our Country

Prang-a-wan part-pak-yoo-a-po
Let's not fight

Moongay-wata laka-n-ngeeye watnanda
Let's talk together

Moongay-wata wanga-kee-wan watnanda
Let's listen together

Yoonggama
Promise, reciprocity, give and receive

Pang ngootee weeng-wanoong
We remember

Wata-wanoong watnanda
We come together

What is kooroondee? What is its meaning? How is it pronounced? Kooroondee: to live in proper relationship; to live in Law; Tyamateeyt; to live in respect. K as in kick, OO as in foot, R as in road, OO as in foot, N as in now, D as in done, EE as in feet. Kooroondee is a word, phrase, semantic domain that resonates in my heart-soul, through my body, in my DNA.

To clarify and give context, Google tells me that definitions of semantic domain include: a specific area of cultural emphasis; a range of potential meanings of a word; an area of meaning and the words used to talk about it.

I speak of semantic domains because kooroondee is not a singular word. It is a phrase, a spectrum of meaning that holds deep knowledge and the concept of 'domain' assists in understanding First Nations languages and meanings.

Some further information is also included below to show some of the ways semantic domains are used to consider and reflect axiological principles of social and cultural value and the context and extent of our cultural ontologies:

> In the social sciences, the concept of semantic domains stemmed from the ideas of cognitive anthropology. The quest was originally to see how the words that groups of humans use to describe

> certain things are relative to the underlying perceptions and meanings that those groups share. (Harriet J Ottenheimer, *The Anthropology of Language*, 2006)

Kooroondee in Cultural Being is in our thinking, our categorisation, the ordering of our world and the assigning of meaning. It is our ontological perspective that is founded in and centres on the principle of inherent interconnectivity of continuing Creation – past, present and future continuum; ever-presence; symbiotic synergistic coexistence – and the positioning and place of Belonging.

Kooroondee is the resonating frequencies and vibratory essence of continuous and concurrent (re)Creation. Kooroondee is to be in proper relationship, to be in your unique Belonging in family and kinship Meerreengee, in Country – Meerreeng Meerreeng, Moornong Meerreeng, Meerteeyt Meerreeng, Ngalam Meen Meerreeng.

Kooroondee in speaking – the experience – the sounds of the word as it rolls across my thalang, reverberating in my ngoolang, vibrating my vocal cords and passing through my wurrung. This voicing of kooroondee evokes a visceral physical response, bringing forth the sounds from my body – in my mouth, feeling the sounds, and then hearing the sounds as they emerge into the world.

As I voice this word, as I repeat kooroondee in a moment or in a chant – the frequency of each sound within kooroondee joins in a symphony of mnemonics, which activates my body on molecular DNA levels of physicality evoking a sense of uplifting, of Belonging in place, time, space.

My spirit, Weerreeyarr/Warrumyeearr, soars in resonance, my heart and mind swell to fullness, completeness, in a knowing of who I am and where I Belong. My body is wired to speak my Mother Tongue; our Country hears our Mother Tongue; Mother Tongue is of Country. It is imperative for the healing of Spirit of Country, of humans and our non-human kin for Mother Tongue to be spoken, to be heard, to be felt.

To sing Country, to dance Country, to paint Country, to feel and be with Country.

PANG-KAPOO-N PANG-KAPOO-K
MEERREENG-NGEEYE

ALWAYS WAS ALWAYS WILL BE
OUR LAND

AND DARK THE NIGHT

Samuel Wagan Watson

SAMUEL WAGAN WATSON hails from the honourable ancestors of the Birra-Gubba, Mununjali, Germanic and Gaelic peoples. His poetry collection, *Of Muse, Meandering and Midnight* won the David Unaipon Award in 1999. He has also written the collections *Hotel Bone*; *Itinerant Blues*; *Smoke Encrypted Whispers*, which won the 2005 New South Wales Premier's Awards Book of the Year and the Kenneth Slessor Prize for Poetry; *The Curse Words*; and *Love Poems and Death Threats*, which won the 2016 Scanlon Award for Indigenous Poetry. In 2018 Samuel was awarded the Patrick White Award.

On the homelands of honourable Gubbi-Gubbi clans, purity of their country turned inside out. Poison the night-shade, black some human conditions. We were raised to respect the borrol – shadow – mighty Tibrogargan and his kin. Nevermore fear necessary, or tough love inflicted for our own good. Duggai – pain like cancer; our Elders camp-light-eyes better than holy water.

Sinister plans brew
Darkness painted in space-dust,
Munnjur screaming …

Wetland blues; menacing-wings whining incessantly, ignoring our own mozzie-coil traps. Blind Willie Johnson wailing charms on Dad's late-night wireless; as fear-fetching as curlew cries after the soul of a man, death comes calling by degrees and taxes, tears and ashes …

Chants from forgotten ghosts verbatim,

And dark the night …

MIRRI

Karlie Noon

KARLIE NOON is a Kamilaroi astronomer, author and science communicator with over a decade of experience advocating for Indigenous inclusion in STEM. Karlie is pursuing a PhD in Astronomy as an Indigenous research associate at the Australian National University.

Mirri's looking down on us,
whispering what it's all about.
Seasons and cycles and dangers,
protecting and guiding when gunni goes down.

I learnt about them when I was little,
sitting by the fire listening to Uncle,
he told us the stars are our kin connecting us to him.

From the centre of a star to the ground to our totems, and to all around the universe, we are a part of one big motion. All expanding outwards, like a dance composed over time, all connected through vivid gold webs that can never be touched or stolen.

When we grow up, we will all be mirris, shining bright and bold, and all the stories we hold. The cousins and relos will hold their heads high, sharing constellations of our kinship to sky. Weaving us to the soil and scrub, and to all the mirri who have died and been reborn up above.

One day, we will all be mirris and sing the songs that we all learnt. That one day it'll be our job to show our babies that caring for Country is our way, and sitting and listening and watching is our strength.

But more and more, our work is getting harder. Things down here are loud and bright and the mirris are getting darker. How can we listen when the stars are too dim? Are we losing our knowledge, our cycles, our songs and our traditions? All we asked is that they tread lightly, but them new mob never listened, just nodded politely.

And now we got fake mirri moving around the sky. They claiming this as their Country but we know it's all gammin – lie on top of lie. Cos these new mirri don't know nothing about the lores of the land.

The ones down here who have claimed all this space, they change the sky and try to sell it back to us, saying, it's all good. That tell us we don't know nothing, and they are fit to be in charge. But their stars are not real cos real mirri can have a laugh. They sit in their place and twinkle and shine. Not these fake mirri though – they just zip on by.

The sky is getting sick with all this new stuff. Just like the land was polluted and grazed, and our rivers turned to dust. And we can't find our stories to find our way home. Cos we all getting sick too, like all this was planned and them new mob approved.

I still pray to the mirri.
To my maran, the Buwadjarr, my gunni, and dhawun,
to sing to the spirits of my babies and ancestors
still searching to find me.

A PARADOX OF EMPOWERMENT

Kim Scott

KIM SCOTT is an award-winning novelist, who has twice won the Miles Franklin Literary Award (for *Benang* and *That Deadman Dance*), along with other Australian literary prizes. Proud to be one among those who call themselves Noongar, Kim is convenor of the Wirlomin Noongar Language and Stories Project, which is responsible for several bilingual (Noongar and English) picture books and many regional performances of story and song (wirlomin.com.au). He is currently Curtin University's Distinguished Professor in the School of Media, Creative Arts and Social Inquiry.

I wanted to refer to a picture that is part of a language project I've worked on for many years now. The picture comes from a story about a Noongar man leaping into a whale. The man chooses to do this. It's no accident – it's not like Jonah in the Bible. He trusts the story his father has given him to such an extent that he is willing to risk his life to make himself a character in its re-enactment, and in the belief that it will expand his world.

I also chose to begin this way because – as the image I'm referring to suggests – it is about seeing things differently. That's what I want to write about: the possibility of seeing things differently through Indigenous language and story 'revitalisation'. So is this an image of a porthole, or is it an eye? In the Noongar language from which this story derives, it's not really clear whether the protagonist is looking through the eye and seeing things differently because of that, or looking with the eye. Has he to some degree become the whale and been transformed through enacting the story?

When I talk about seeing things differently, I don't necessarily mean some sort of binary opposition, but more of an expansion of ways of seeing – some growth from where we are now, from where we begin. This is a contemporary image, but it is from an ancient story, a Creation Story in an ancient language emerging from a small Aboriginal community organisation – the Wirlomin Noongar Language and Stories Project – based on the south coast of Western Australia.

I particularly want to discuss the endeavour of language recovery and what it might add to our sense of identity and belonging, as a member of both a particular Indigenous community and the wider nation-state of Australia. Let me begin with an example, if not of alphabets and stories on paper, then of semantic markings made in sand early in our shared history. I suggest it offers a primary or fundamental description of how we are positioned today, of where our shared language has stranded us.

It's 1788. Governor Arthur Phillip enters Sydney Harbour with three small boats; longboats they called them, not even the great billowing sails of empire, because the ships have stayed in Botany Bay and the governor is having a sniff around to see if he can find a better place to stake his claim. He's repeatedly told to go away, people shake spears at him, dance to make him disappear. But then this very strange thing happens … (I must tell you I take great pride in these moments, even though they're politically awkward) … some Aboriginal men wade out to the boat, and they guide him into a little cove, perhaps because they're madly curious about what's going on, perhaps to confront and control him. And there is the fascinating cross-cultural encounter on the beaches that many historians have remarked upon.

There was exchange and trade and, as author and historian Inga Clendinnen has emphasised, there was also much dancing. In this particular instance there was also a bit of jostling and poking, along with the examination of teeth and nostrils and much pulling at clothing. In fact, this all apparently got to be a bit too much for Governor Arthur Phillip and his men. Phillip writes:

> as their curiosity made them very troublesome when we were preparing our dinner I made a circle around us. There was little difficulty in making them understand that they were not to come within it and they then sat down very quiet. (Keith Vincent Smith, *Bennelong: The coming in of the Eora*, 2001)

His men and their cooking fire remain inside the circle that Phillip has drawn in the sand. Things are suddenly no longer so convivial. Phillip and his party are no longer so open to curiosity and sharing. They have seen it necessary to 'draw a line in the sand'. It bears some thinking about this story, I think. It tells of exclusion and of an enforced power relationship, which is a very familiar motif in our shared history.

You might remember a song from some years ago: 'Treaty'. Remember the line 'Promises can disappear just like writing in the sand'? I'm not sure that this particular line – Governor Phillip's line in the sand – has disappeared. Even though it may be emblematic of our history, it certainly needn't be permanent – it too can disappear. However, to date, such an insistence on power over and exclusion of Aboriginal people seems a defining feature of Australian identity.

What was being excluded from that circle? I'm thinking of knowledge such as that outlined in Bill Gammage's wonderful book *The Biggest Estate on Earth*. Gammage writes about 'firestick farming', in which Aboriginal people deployed fire across the continent with complexity and skill 'greater than anything modern Australia has imagined'. This was kept outside of the circle way back then, and perhaps ever since.

Gammage talks about how 'a mobile people organised a continent with precision. They sanctioned key principles, think long-term, leave the world as it is, think globally, act locally. They were active, not passive, striving for balance and continuity to make all life abundant, convenient and predictable.' An ethos of sustainability, we might say. And he talks about how the many Indigenous cultures across the nation enabled an abundance that allowed for a 'voluminous and intricate spiritual and creative practice'.

In another rigorous study, *A Place for Strangers: Towards a history of Australian Aboriginal being*, Tony Swain explains an Indigenous worldview that prioritises place instead of time. It is not necessarily accurate to describe this as 'cyclical', he says, because a circle is just a line eating itself. Instead, such a worldview relies on a sense of rhythmic patterns in the landscape. Place consciousness relies on an awareness of rhythms like those of the moon, of the sun, of the rhythms of tides, of the wind, and all the very many rhythms of place, of its plants flowering and spilling their seeds, of gestation and birth and death.

In the northern hemisphere a cultural renaissance blossomed from people digging up shards of pottery and broken statues and recovering ancient languages. What about here, in the south, in Australia? What might it mean to not just recover bits and pieces, not just fragments of pottery and broken statues, but to recover the language and stories of even greater antiquity and that are part of the structure and rhythm of the landscape we inhabit? They are surely a major denomination in the currency of identity and belonging. And how do we recover them ethically, without confirming the power imbalance and theft that characterise so much of Australia's relationship with its Aboriginal peoples?

I've mentioned language and heritage as powerful cultural sources and suggested they mostly exist outside the circle of Australian society. But those neglected, marginalised cultural sources are in danger. The circle of Governor Arthur Phillip has expanded, and the world outside of it, in some ways, has shrunk because of the fundamentals of our history: stolen Country, a tiny percentage of the original population surviving the first decades of colonisation, and then an apartheid-like regime intended to crush people and their culture and language.

My chief concern is one endangered dialect of the language indigenous to south-western Australia – Noongar language – my ancestral tongue. The Wirlomin Noongar Language and Stories Project is a community-based cultural organisation and is about recovering, reconnecting and rebuilding a pre-colonial heritage of language, story and connection to Country. It is about consolidating that source, and using it to gather momentum to, perhaps paradoxically, propel us into the future. A better future.

Aunty Hazel Brown and her siblings have been key figures in this. The Wirlomin Noongar Language and Stories Project partly began with a book we did together – *Kayang & Me*. It became obvious to us when we were writing it that, for a whole range of reasons, her knowledge and values weren't being transmitted to – and consolidated in – our little home community, let alone anywhere else. We wanted that heritage consolidated there – in its home community – first. It can heal us, the different sense of identity you get from the old stories and songs rather than from language and narrative emanating from shared history and the coloniser's perspective, and then, especially if others – including the colonisers, those inside the circle – have an appetite for such material, one can also be empowered through the act of sharing. It's a thing to do carefully, I suggest, but when done well it can mean a transformation of relationships, including that between those within and outside the circle.

We started by bringing people – extended family, community – together, and holding 'workshops' to explore and play with the language Aunty Hazel and her siblings and cousins carried. And we also brought various fragments of our ancestral language, collected from a range of archival sources and informants, to these gatherings. This developed into a sequence of workshops, each with a slightly different focus. Sometimes, I fear, it can seem a bit teacherly, all of us in a room looking at bits of paper. Other times there'll be a range of us around a campfire: different generations, different ages, different families.

The first time we got together like this was around 2006, and we were returning archival material to the descendants of a particular linguist's 'informants'. The material had been collected in 1930 in Albany. We pulled together the children or, in some cases, the grandchildren of the people who'd given words and stories to the linguist. We wanted to pull them out in front of a group and say here's your dad's stuff, here's your granddad's stuff, here's your uncle's stuff. It's yours, and we've got some ideas for how we'd like to work on it together. But before we got to that, and within five minutes of beginning, everyone in the room was crying, and the old ones were saying, 'We only get together like this at funerals these days.'

The emotional intensity took us all by surprise, and was to do with the very business of reconnecting and the possibility that we could listen to those old people again. It was they who had brought us together, and these stories and language were right at the heart of us. It was wonderful. And it continues to be wonderful, people getting together around our old people and their language.

As some might know, communities – particularly oppressed communities – can sometimes be fiercely political and riven with factions and rivalries. We've had people contact us, and they're hurt and cranky. 'What are you doing – that's my family's material you're working with.' Words like that. And we've invited them along to join us and all shared the pleasure and realisation that they too are necessary to what we are doing. Stories grow stronger from being shared.

Thus in recent years we've had material donated from older members of extended family. Sometimes it's what might be regarded as scraps, fragments, jottings, poor audio recordings. Sometimes it's come from an official archive. Often, some of us will read it aloud. It's not unusual for someone to speak up and say, 'You don't say it like that,' or, 'You say it like this,' or just, 'No, no.' But people will also offer, 'I know another story like that' or they'll remember the informants or share some other things they've remembered. So, in fact, we're adding value to and supplementing the 'archive' and we're escaping the binary of paper archival history versus oral history. And we begin to develop stories out of these fragments and cross-reference what different individuals know with what the paperwork tells us.

So it's consolidation first. Material being returned and consolidated in self-drawn, small circles before being gradually shared from that same centre in ever-widening circles, that can again shrink back to the centre in order to reassure and comfort and 'own'. Then expand again.

I want to share a couple of words from people involved with the Wirlomin Noongar Language and Stories Project. These examples are from people taking part in presentations we do at schools that feature our stories, songs and process. Connie Moses said:

> I'm just so proud to be part of the journey. We are a team, you know, and we're growing together. I just can't wait to get up and dance and sing. It's just so wonderful to hear everyone speak, especially the Elders.

Russell Nelly, an Elder who is no longer with us, said:

> I want to tell you, it's a privilege to share what we feel with the kids. I get emotional at times but when I get emotional I'm listening to the old fellas because they're talking to me along with them talking to you guys. Prior to this I was lost, I had circumnavigated Australia three times looking for my identity and it brought me all the way back to Katanning. I heard of the Wirlomin mob. I thought, no, they don't want me. That's all changed now. We've got something tangible. I always tell you, we've got something tangible. What we've lost we are resurrecting.

I hope you can see the possibilities of healing and transformation from reconnecting in this way with a pre-colonial heritage. Done in the way I have described – firstly consolidated and enhanced in its home community – our heritage of language, story and song can heal and empower us. The force of these old narratives – the absence of the evils that follow colonisation, the identities and trajectories they offer – can both heal and offer alternative narratives. And we are further empowered by also sharing, and being in control of the sharing, aspects of our heritage. It can be a surprise for some of us to realise non-Aboriginal people are increasingly hungry for this material, and willing to give us space and their ears and interest.

Our intangible and diverse Aboriginal heritages are major denominations in the currency of identity and belonging. I use such terminology in order to tiptoe towards legislative and political discourse, and the language of money and funding. Cultural capital. We need to find ways to invest in this together. It might even be, may I suggest, a matter of compounding interest.

LEARNING BUNDJALUNG ON THARAWAL

Evelyn Araluen

EVELYN ARALUEN is a poet, researcher and co-editor of *Overland*. Her widely published criticism, fiction and poetry has been awarded the Nakata Brophy Short Fiction and Poetry Prize for Young Indigenous Writers, the Judith Wright Poetry Prize, a Wheeler Centre Next Chapter Fellowship and a Neilma Sidney Literary Travel Fund grant. Evelyn's collection *Dropbear* was shortlisted for the 2021 Judith Wright Calanthe Award for a Poetry Collection and the 2022 Kenneth Slessor Prize for Poetry, and won the 2022 Stella Prize. Born and raised on Dharug Country, she is a descendant of the Bundjalung Nation.

Above his desk it is written:
I wish I knew the names of all the birds.

I know this room through tessellation of leaf and branch,
wurahŋ-bil and jaran-gir,
in the shade of a kulsetsi –
(Cherokee) 'honey locust' [a flowering tree]

I am relearning these hills and saltwaters
and all the places wrapped around this room
we both have dagahral here,
lovers/fathers/friends/conquerors/
ghosts

But here, in this new and ancient place,
I ask him to name the song that swoops through this
mosaic:

sometimes it is wattlebird sometimes it is currawong –
when we drive, he tells me king parrot, fairy wren,
  black cockatoo

and I know jalwahn and bilin bilin and ngarehr
          but the rest are just nunganybil,
          the rest are just: 'bird'

It is hard to unlearn a language:
          to unspeak the empire,
          to teach my voice to rise and fall like landscape,
a topographic intonation

So in this place the shape of my place
I am trying to sing like hill and saltwater,
to use old words from old country I am so far from:
          bundjalung jagum ngai, nganduwal nyuyaya,
and god, I don't even know
                    if I'm saying it right

But I watch the bark twist:
grey and slate and vanilla and vermilion
                    he tells me this is ribbon gum –
so I find five words for this bark
and I promise I will learn them all

Because to hold him is to hold the tree
that holds these birds I cannot name,
and a word spoken here
might almost sound like home

We are relearning this place through poetry:
I open my book and say, wayan,
here is a word which means road, but also root
and in it I am rooted, earthed,
singing between two lands
I learn that balun is both river and milky way,
and that he is baray-gir, the youngest child
and the top of the tree,
where the gahr will come to rest –
to call its own name
across the canopy,
long after his word for it
is gone.

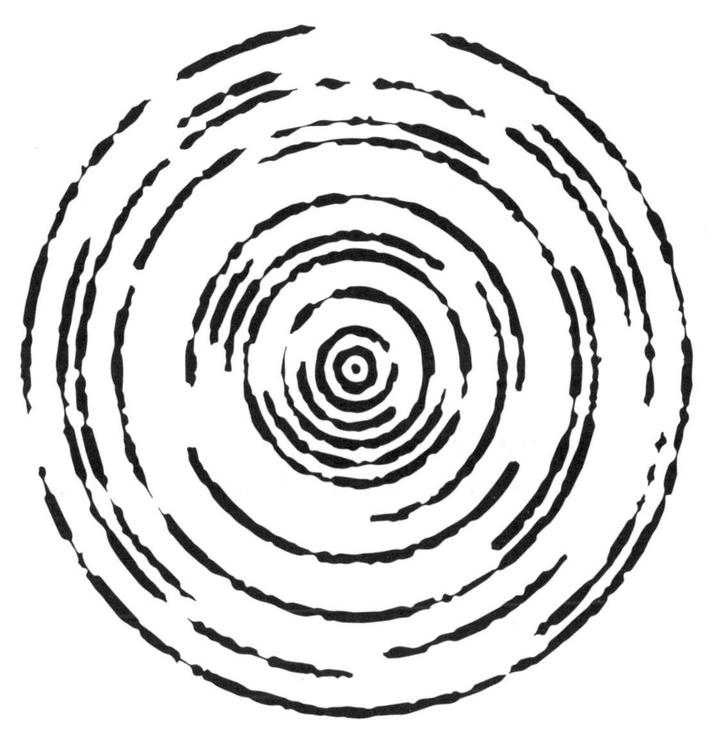

NGALIIBULANYUGIYAN(BA)

Merinda Dutton

MERINDA DUTTON is a Gumbaynggirr and Barkindji woman and emerging First Nations writer, critic and the co-founder of Blackfulla Bookclub, an online community for First Nations stories. In 2019 Merinda was recognised for her legal aid work with Aboriginal community and awarded the National Indigenous Legal Professional of the Year.

We two, mother and daughter (a pair)
Nganyundi Buwarr,
My baby. Ngaaja ngiina ganggurrinymang.
I dreamt you.

I dreamt you up and somehow you are more vivid than I ever imagined. You were once just a wish and, in a world made up of miraculous events, you junuy, are a miracle. Maybe one day I'll tell you about it and our journey to becoming ngaliibulanyugiyan(ba). I gift you these words and memories now, even though I know you do not comprehend them yet. May the knowledge of our kinship be a talisman of love you carry with you throughout your life.

It is autumn now and the wind whispers to us both in conspiracy, reminding us that the cool season approaches. You don't seem to mind about the wind though. In fact, you lick your lips as if to taste the air.

It seems delicious to you. In the mornings, your magpie relatives greet you in song. You reply with your own sweet melody.

You are learning to roll over and soon you will be learning to crawl, and then to stand. I try to hold on to these small moments, but they seem to slip out of my mind's grasp like sand in making way for new memories and realities. Our days are milk-soaked entanglements. We chase sleep where we can. With each new sunrise, I see a new side of you. As the sun sets, new versions of me emerge too.

Somewhere between the before and now, I've developed a sixth sense for you. I can hear you across the wind and white noise, accessing a soundwave known only to us and unlocked by our mutual DNA. There was once a time I slept through all manner of sounds. These days, my ears are hyper-attuned to your unique vibration. I wake at a mere inkling of you. Invisible tethers of life float between us, linking us. Our bond is an ancient one, embodied synchronicity, reminding us that there is nothing new under the sun. I suppose this is what it means to be we two, bulanyugiyan(ba).

We are learning about each other each day. And yet, we aren't. We have done this before, been here before. A thousand mothers and daughters before us breathe into our existence. Our back-family love on to us, guiding us through our journey on this plane. I feel them surrounding us, I see them in your face.

Meeting you is to remember myself, and us. Listening to my intuition is to hear an echo of an older iteration of us – from a time before time. Ngaliibulanyugiyan(ba).

Motherhood feels like good community and loving relations. It is the richness of being held and of holding, all at once. And yet, I am not one mother alone. I am one of many. You are lucky, junuy, to have many mothers. Communal love and matriarchy surrounds you, embracing and enriching your spirit. My two sisters, who you will also come to call miimi(ga), will be there for you – to care for you, teach you and instil values in you. They will protect you.

You have many other relatives too, daughter – human and non-human. Remember nyugiyan, we are kinfolk with the land, waters and sky. We are connected to all things. This is the manner of Gumbaynggirr relationality that will be the blueprint for you and your reality, as it has been for mine. Indeed, it is this tradition of reciprocal relations that has been the foundation of our ongoing existence and subsistence in this place. Through and because of it, we are still here.

The threads of our lives entwine us in an ancient story – one that will be repeated long after we are gone from this place. We are woven together – nganyundi buwarr – a tapestry of kinship, Country and lore. While there are times that our stories will diverge from each other, you will not be alone on your path. You are from and of this land. This is an important truth for your journey here. Hold on to it, fiercely.

Ngaliibulanyugiyan(ba).

—

GUMBAYNGGIRR WORDS

Bula – two
Bulanyugiyan(ba) – pair of mother & daughter, or father & daughter
Buwarr – baby
Ganggurriny – dream
Junuy – little, small or child
Miimi(ga)/miimi – mother, also refer to mother's sister
Ngaaja ngiina ganggurrinymang – I dreamt you, I dreamt about you
Nganyundi – my
Ngalii – we two, you and I
Nyugiyan – daughter

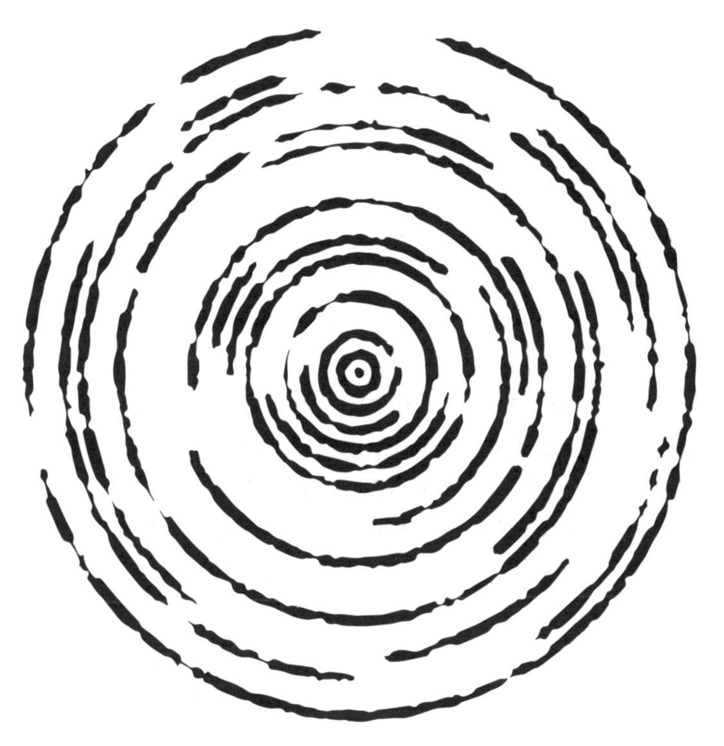

TIDDA

Yasmin Smith

YASMIN SMITH is a poet and editor of South Sea Islander, Kabi Kabi, Northern Cheyenne and English heritage. Her poetry has featured in *Meanjin*, *Overland*, *Australian Poetry Journal*, *Island*, *Best of Australian Poems*, *Griffith Review* and more. She has been shortlisted for the Judith Wright Poetry Prize, and she won the Gwen Harwood Poetry Prize and Varuna's First Nations Flagship Fellowship in 2024. She is UQP's series editor of the First Nations Classics and works across fiction, non-fiction, children's books and poetry.

tingira tidda
wades at the timbers
in the mouth of an estuary
shaped like a moonbeam

gouged in the foot-pockets
of spongey shivered sapwood
bowed by wet bodies,
tidda's body sings

how are we to see her
blossoming limbs to the
brackish currents,
her fingertips spun
by seagrass strings

tidda returns to
drowned river-valley,
tidda becomes nestled
in holy tendrils of algae

tidda sinks in cavities
to the mangroved-deep,
as moon jellies swarm
beneath the newly redeemed

—

My grandmother's language sits on the back of my tongue like pale honey. I haven't quite learnt how to speak her words, yet I know someday I will swallow them sweet. So I choose a word, instead, that has swirled between the many generations of my sister-cousins and sissys and aunties. A word we have always shared in comfort and community: tidda or tidda-girl. A word that weaves us tightly to the truth of who we belong to. Reminding me of who I am tied to by blood, by spirit, by bone.

When I was a child, tidda would come with a string of laughter as my mother would playfully say: *hey tidda, here tidda, where you going, tidda-girl?* I never knew the weight of this word until I watched her passing, surrounded by daughters, by sisters, by aunties. Tidda holds joy and grief. Tidda holds all the women who I have never met or am yet to meet or will someday meet again: my great-grandmothers swimming from islet to island, my mother gathering stars above moonlit-sea, my grandmothers wading in saltwater creeks.

I think of the universality of our languages that tow meaning into understanding, like the evening moon tugging the tide into early dawn. I think of the brief moment I walked by Thelma Plum on a sidewalk café in West End: *hey sis*, she says. I text my tiddas: *you'll never guess who I just saw on the street!* Tidda captures our bonds of acknowledgement but it also welcomes the newness of connection. Too often tidda is unspoken because as language spins us together – relationally, spiritually, metaphorically – it does so by an unvoiced invitation of acceptance and the reciprocity of being received. Tidda is in the exchange and in the gifting.

I think of the tiddas I have read in stories, like May in Tara June Winch's *Swallow the Air.* Of the time my mother and I wept in the dark at the cinema as we watched Molly and Daisy and Gracie, three tiddas return home across Country, trekking through sprawls of desert-flower in *Rabbit-Proof Fence.* I admire the tiddas who have handwoven our histories into baskets and bangles and dillybags. These strong lineages of sisterhood – stroked into paintings – in the lapse of time and dance, in ceremony, in celebration.

When I listen to traditional language being sung or spoken or shared I am stirred by all of this sovereignty, embodied and owned, by First Nations creators. We ode ourselves to those around us, to the generations before and to those who may come.

But in truth, this word makes me think of my closest. Of the sister who I have left, now that my mother has gone. Tidda, my sister, I cannot think of a better world to swim in if you were not here in sunlight and song.

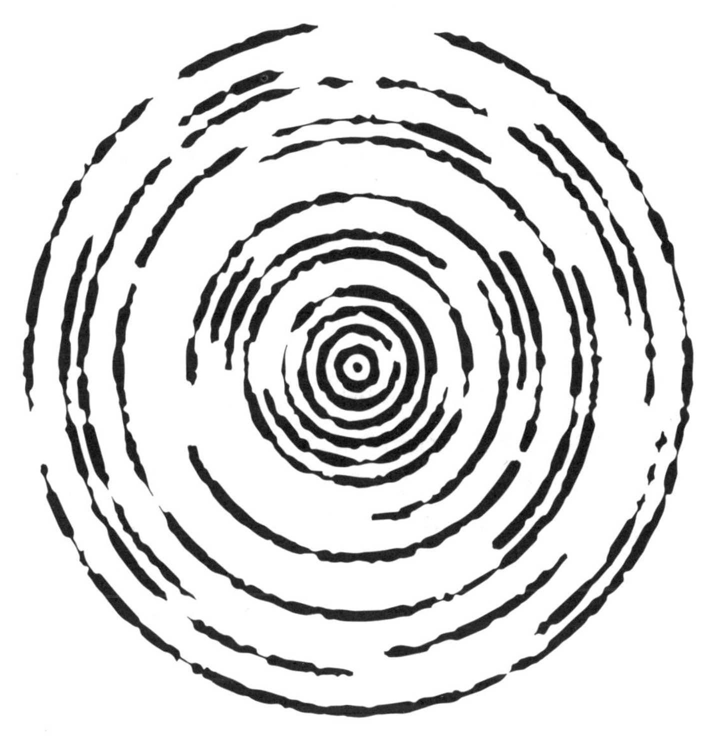

BINGYADYAN GNALLU BIRRUNG NUDJARN JUNGARUNG

Bruce Pascoe

BRUCE PASCOE has published widely in both adult and young adult literature. He has won numerous awards, including the Children's Book Council of Australia Eve Pownall Award for *Young Dark Emu*, NSW Premier's Literary Awards Book of the Year for *Dark Emu*, and the Prime Minister's Literary Award for young adult literature for *Fog a Dox*. In 2018 Bruce was awarded the Australia Council Award for Lifetime Achievement in Literature. Bruce is a Yuin, Bunurong and Tasmanian man, and currently lives on his farm in Gippsland, Victoria.

Bingyadyan gnallu birrung nudjarn jungarung is a Yuin phrase that means 'we all rise from the mother's heartbeat'. Yuin men are obliged to begin a formal conversation with a phrase like 'through the mother', Bingyadyan gnallu birrung nudjarn jungarung. And they're obliged to end that conversation the same way, 'through the mother'.

We walk the mountain – my daughter, my wife, my grandson – and it is there where we go through a section of Yuin law. Yuin law is all about women, and when you walk through the law, you pass by Nyardi, the first woman. She's a huge granite tower and Tunkoo, the man, is a tiny fellow.

Men have to restrain their ego a little bit because this is what it's all about, it's where it comes from – it's through the mother. And then you see the passage through lore of any person on Earth and it's always through the mother. You see Nyardi pregnant and you're invited to put your hand on Nyardi's belly – one of the most intimate things you could ever do in life. Some men struggle with that, not having been used to touching women in that way, and it's a salutary lesson that we make all young men do, and those who can't will have to wait.

Then you see the child on Nyardi's back, then you see the whole history of mankind in three rocks: the past, the present and the future. Then you see the birth canal and the baby and there are other features too. But when you leave that area the thing that impresses you – especially if you have been to art galleries, churches, war memorials, great public features of the parliament of any nation – is that you will realise that you have seen no weapon. And you will realise that no other country on Earth is like this.

This is a great lesson that the world should know and sadly Australia has not paid credence to their first culture. The world is begging for an answer to the problem of violence and the answer is Bingyadyan gnallu birrung nudjarn jungarung.

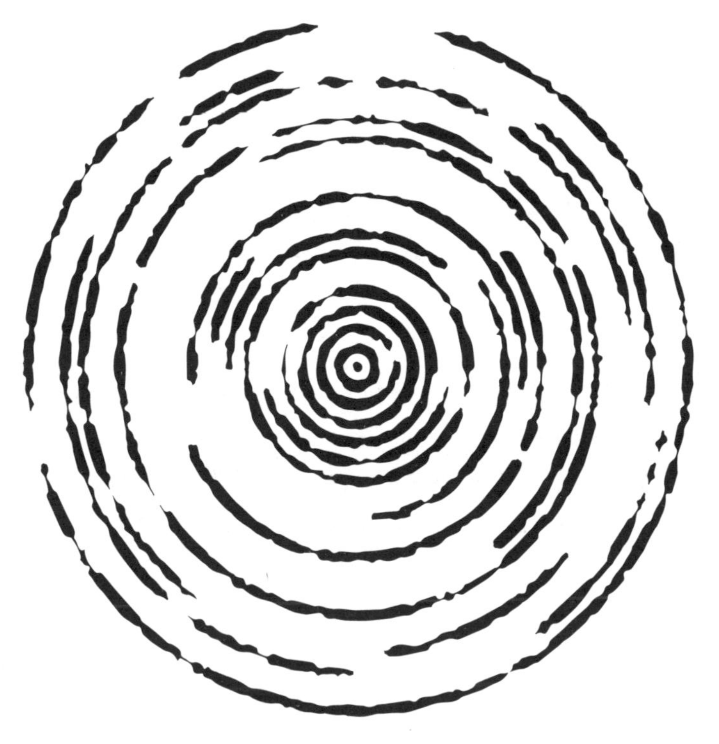

WAARKI

Jack Latimore

JACK LATIMORE is a Birpai–Thungutti man based on Boon Wurrung Country in Melbourne. He is the Aboriginal Affairs journalist for *The Age* and has previously worked for *The Guardian* and SBS NITV.

The skinned man was the first devil-spirit to visit me. It was the late 1970s, my father was in the army, and my mother, baby brother and I lived in an outer Sydney suburb and alone for most of the time. Or so it seemed.

I first saw him slip across our short hallway between bedrooms one night. I was on my way to the bathroom at the back of the house to brush my teeth and, in one of those moments where you can't be sure if you saw something or not, I caught a glimpse of him.

It was just a flicker of movement, a flash of his lower leg and foot vanishing into the doorway of a darkened room. Screaming, I scarpered back down the hall into the front room. My mother was drinking coffee even though it was night. She was by the front window that looked out onto the street and the big tree in the front yard that shed ruby-red leaves in the autumn. In the night, it was half illuminated by the streetlights.

The skinned man materalised again before dawn, just when the little birds begin to chitter. He crawled through my bedroom window. This memory has stuck with me the longest.

He dragged me out of my little bed and planted me in the front car of a rollercoaster. The skeletal track curled and corkscrewed all around our little fibro house, snaking in and out of windows, scooping in and out of doorways, coiling high above the big deciduous tree.

We tore away, casting off metallic sparks. My neck cricked as we careened around the track jolting this way, that way. The wheels screeched and shrieked. And all the while, the skinned man grinned silently at me. Right there in my face, row upon row of pointy, serrated teeth receding from the front of his mouth back into his raw gullet.

The horror stayed with me for decades longer than it should have. Much longer than the second devil-spirit that spooked me. That poor fella may as well have been the soft moon appearing from behind a trail of midnight cloud in comparison. That's just the way it goes with devil-spirits – some bite, others not quite.

But then came the Waarki.

Ahead of writing this piece down, I asked my brother-boys two things: did they ever have a brush with the Waarki; could they tell me about it if they had?

We're all in our late thirties and early forties now. We have our own children, professional jobs, monthly rent or mortgages to pay. Some of us have grown bald, some carry too much weight or suffer lower back pain; we struggle with bad habits, with dialling our racing thoughts down at night to find enough hours of sleep.

'Stop talking about it, fuck ya,' the eldest of us pleaded. 'I'm getting goosebumps here now, look. Don't even mention the fucking thing.'

But I'm a journalist and my curiosity grabbed me, was dragging me about, saying more words that probably shouldn't be said, and you know the old adage about curiosity. Some say the Waarki's legs bend backwards like a bird. Some say he has red eyes. Some say the Waarki has feet like a goat. Some are adamant that he works for the hairy men. Others say he is hairy himself and works for the featherfoot fellas. Some say the gitja bird works for him.

If I transport myself back in time, to my early life, I hear my great-great-grandmother warn me about him. I smell her kerosene heater burning in the small lounge room closed against the night.

'Don't go outside or the Waarki will get hold of you, boy.' Her voice is commanding even in memory.

And as my age flutters forward, I hear little nan – my great-grandmother – warn me about the Waarki too. Then it's my big nan, and my mother. The Waarki is suddenly ever-present in my waking life, in all my worlds of being.

Not just me either. All the cousins, brothers, sisters face the prospect of the Waarki in the daylight and night dark of their childhoods. And the Waarki is an especially threatening presence when all of us are together at the big family celebrations or Sorry Business. Its wrath and bloody appetite increase according to our number.

As a young man relocated north of our homeland, I was walking home one night along Letitia Road in Fingal towards my uncle and aunty's place when I spotted the Waarki hunched near a headstone in the old boneyard between the road and the beach. I burst into a frantic sprint. In my panic, the only thought was my uncle's advice to me when I moved in: if any spirit from outside tried to get me, then run inside his house as fast as possible, because he'd sung a protector spirit into the house.

'When will the Waarki ever stop?' I despaired at the time.

I looked up 'Waarki' in the Gathang dictionary put together years ago by the Muurrbay Aboriginal Language and Culture Co-operative in Nambucca Heads. I didn't see it. The dictionary covers three dialects of our First Language, but the Waarki is elusive. I tried to identify different spellings of the word, thinking maybe it was a derivative and I found Djagiri (devil-spirit), Guwiyn (ghost-spirit), Dulagal (spirit), Goonj (evil spirit, big hairy man) and Goi-on (a devil-monster who deals out punishment).

I messaged my aunty-cousin and cousin-sister who both work in the restoration and community renewal of our traditional language. I knew they'd both felt the Waarki lurking in their lives. They were around plenty of times when the old nans raised the Waarki alarm. I asked why the word is not in the dictionary and they both told me it was likely from elsewhere and was socialised into our people when we were impounded on the missions and government reserves.

I began to understand the Waarki is also white. But where did this devil-spirit spring from? Where was its headwater, its roots?

My cousin-sister pledged to wiggle it out of her language archive, but for now speculates that it could likely come from north or north-west of our people.

Then I was on a job, thousands of kilometres from Country, and I saw an old man monitoring the frequency emitted from a fallen scar tree. The body of the tree was the centrepiece of a new exhibit in an influential white institution and the old man had travelled down from Gomeroi lands to attend the launch. I asked him if the Waarki is from out his way. He quit scanning the cultural markings on the tree with his hands and scrutinised me for a moment.

'Yes, from the fringe of the desert, it comes from the south-west of my Country,' he said. 'He is one of the hybrid people who came down from the sky to scuff the children up.'

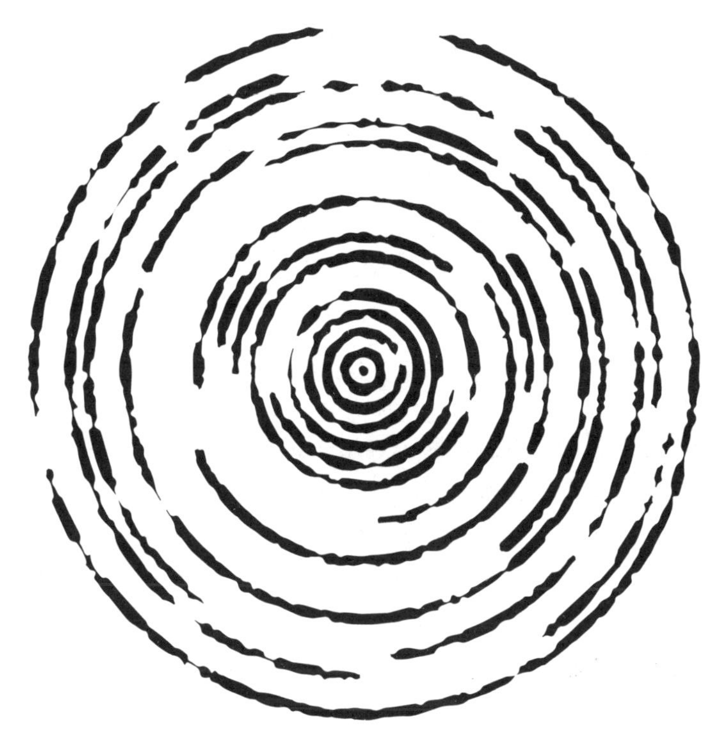

BALARR

Jenna Lee

JENNA LEE is a Gulumerridjin (Larrakia), Wardaman and KarraJarri Saltwater woman with mixed Japanese, Chinese, Filipino and Anglo-Australian ancestry who uses art to explore and celebrate her many overlapping identities. With a practice focused on materiality and ancestral material culture, she works with notions of the archive, histories of colonial collecting, and settler-colonial books and texts. Jenna ritualistically analyses, deconstructs and reconstructs source material, language and books, transforming them into new forms of cultural beauty and pride, and presenting a tangibly translated form.

Nestled among the poorly formatted Word document containing translations of Gulumerridjin (Larrakia) words into English, the word Balarr appears three times.

Balarr	verb	become light (to –
Balarr	verb	dawn (to –
Balarr	verb	light up (to –

In this listing of words, compiled from anthropologists' documents, the translations of Balarr sit separated, presented in alphabetical order of their English 'meanings'.

To understand the weight of the variations, we must first understand the history of the act of translation. In the late 1800s there was a flurry of activity by anthropologists and linguists to document Aboriginal languages on the perceived brink of death through government-enforced linguicide. The act of listing with such little detail seemingly condemned our languages to a lifetime of isolation from the world that surrounded them, from their people, from their ecosystems and from their right to be alive, to be known, understood and spoken.

However, within this process, Balarr stands as somewhat of an outlier. Its significance exists in the spaces between the translations, offering subtle variations that hold valuable information. In a bitter twist, the very documents that are so painfully void of details are the same ones we use to begin the work of re-knowing. The anthropologists and linguists who recorded these nuances inadvertently gifted us with a starting point for inquiry. What lies in the gaps between 'become light', 'dawn', and 'light up'?

Through years of artistic exploration, using light as a medium to illuminate spaces, I have attempted to distil the essence of Balarr, trying to grasp its original meaning. While I cannot claim a definitive conclusion, I have come to a visceral, deeply personal understanding – a sensation that resonates within my body – and interpretation of what Balarr was and is.

To me, Balarr embodies the fleeting moment when the sun gently emerges over the horizon, painting Gulumerridjin Country with its warm glow. It encapsulates the transformative experience of the sun's rays tickling your skin, as the coolness of the night gives way to the humidity of the day. Balarr is the stirring into consciousness to witness the changing colours of the land – it is a feeling of beginning a new day filled with purpose and tasks to be accomplished.

In its essence, Balarr represents time, manifested through the radiant beams of the sun.

By unravelling the multifaceted layers of Balarr, I reclaim a connection to the roots of Gulumerridjin culture and language. It allows me to appreciate the intricate interplay between nature, the land and my ancestral experiences. On a broader level, this understanding unveils the inherent value of preserving Indigenous languages, not merely as linguistic artefacts, but as conduits to comprehend the world in ways that other languages may not know.

The repetitions and variations of Balarr serve as a reminder of the depth and complexity embedded within Gulumerridjin language. They prompt us to challenge the limitations of translation, calling us to delve deeper into the stories, meanings and connections hidden within the margins.

In this pursuit, Balarr becomes not just a word but a catalyst for reclaiming lost connections, reviving cultural heritage and honouring the wisdom embedded within ancestral languages. It invites us to explore the spaces between translations – where illuminated understanding awaits – and where the stories of the past shape the way we navigate the present.

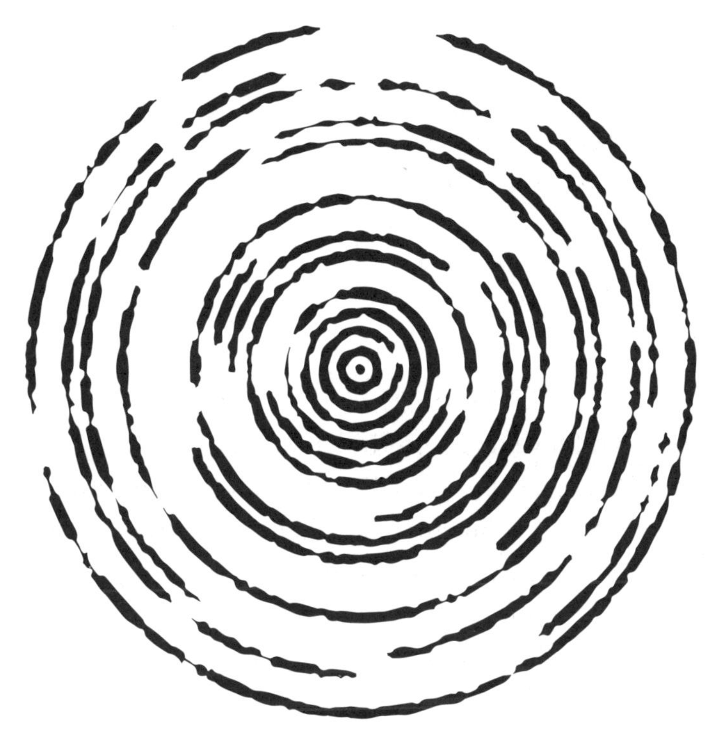

GUGARRA

Jacob Morris

JACOB MORRIS is a proud Gammēya-D̲arrawal man from Shoalhaven on the south-east coast of New South Wales. Jacob is the CPO of Gadhungal Murring, an Indigenous company that focuses on Aboriginal education, language revival and learning, teaching and performing traditional song and dance, consultancy, and tourism. Jacob is a Language Custodian, cultural educator, traditional singer and dancer, mentor, tour guide and poet. His poems are mostly written in his language, Gammēya-D̲arrawal.

Gugarra
Kookaburra

Gu-gu-ga-ga-ga-rra-rra
Gu-gu-ga-ga-ga-rra-rra

Yanaŋu bunwurri, Gugarra djendjembēn
When it's sunrise, Kookaburra laughs.

Yanaŋu darabināgin, Gugarra djendjembēn
When it's the last rays of the sunset, Kookaburra laughs.

Balin-gaḏāŋ ḏadjam yanaŋu bandā ŋiagāŋ,
ŋiagāŋ-guli Bābāŋ ballaiya.
The worst time I was a boy, my Father died.

Dugērri dugērri-billa ŋiagāŋ yagun yindi kuragia,
I cried and cried then you called out.

Bābamarra yagaḏa, Ŋara ŋara nānḏarra
Uncle said, 'Listen listen, look there.'

Ŋaraḏagambala djendjembēn, niara Gugarra
'You can hear laughter, look there Kookaburra.'

Yendāgawa ŋiagāŋ-guli Bābāŋ,
nadaji ŋiagāŋ-guli budjāŋ.
My Father is gone, my bird arrives.

Yanaŋu bunwurri, Gugarra djendjembēn
When it's sunrise, Kookaburra laughs.

Yanaŋu darabināgin, Gugarra djendjembēn
When it's the last rays of sunset, Kookaburra laughs.

Gu-gu-ga-ga-ga-rra-rra
Gu-gu-ga-ga-ga-rra-rra

—

For me, the word Gugarra is a perfect representation of our language. Although I am pretty biased as Gugarra is my bird, what we call 'Budjāŋgul', which actually means I belong to him. He chose me. Ever since my father took his journey (passed away), Gugarra has always been there for me, guiding me physically, spiritually, mentally and emotionally. Dedicating a poem in his name is one of the ways I can give thanks to that special bird.

We did not name the Kookaburra. He named himself. He introduces himself every sunrise and every sunset and every time he laughs. Gugarra is a family bird who not only has a mother and a father, sons and daughters, but also aunties and uncles, cousins and nieces and nephews. They all have a strong bond and responsibility for each other.

The word Gugarra is an example of how our language comes from the land, just like us, just like everything. The land, plants and animals have always been our teachers, so it's safe to say they taught us language as well. Our language is like the stitches in the possum skin cloak. Language connects us to our family, community and Country. We need to be proud of our language, to speak it loud with family, from sunrise to sunset, everyday, just like Gugarra laughs.

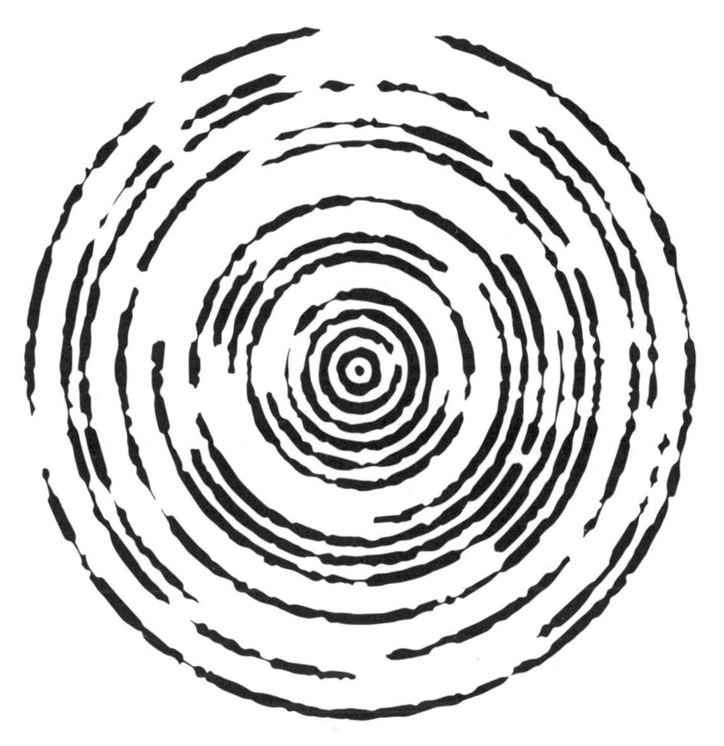

YILAALU

Nardi Simpson

NARDI SIMPSON is a Yuwaalaraay storyteller from New South Wales's north-west freshwater plains. As a member of Indigenous duo Stiff Gins, Nardi has travelled nationally and internationally for the past twenty-five years. She is also a founding member of Freshwater, an all-female vocal ensemble formed to revive the language and singing traditions of New South Wales river communities. Nardi's debut novel, *Song of the Crocodile*, won the 2017 black&write! Fellowship, the Australian Literature Society Gold Medal and was longlisted for the 2021 Stella Prize and Miles Franklin Literary Award.

Yuwaalaraay Country is flat. Our homelands are commonly referred to as the north-west slopes and plains. For me, it is a place of great beauty. And contradiction. It is a place where the red-dirt soil of the west collides with the darker, richer soils of the south – their impact creating magnificence – hot springs and opal abounding beneath the surface. Yuwaalaraay is the site of a system of inland lakes, Dharriwaa – great gathering and teaching and celebration places – where half a million pelicans breed and hatch and a wedge-tailed shares a nest with a sea eagle. It's a place created by a crocodile, their opalised teeth showing how long they have been gone from our plains.

Yuwaalaraay is also a place where rivers gush from the north, creating, in times of abundance, a flood plain that spans the length and breadth of my homelands. This flood plain with its series of gullies, rivers and lakes holds water for weeks during flood. This is known to us as burrul warrambool, the big milky way – a time when earth becomes sky as stars twinkle upon the ground. Yuwaalaraay is floodplain. It also cradles the dry, and drought is a far too regular occurrence in our freshwater home. This is my ngurrumbaa – my homelands. I am from, of and within it, always. It makes me, and I become it, with each breath and step and day. Yuwaalaraay, Dharriwaaga giirr, gubiyaanha ngaya yilaaluga.

In Yuwaalaraay, in places such as Dharriwaa, I swim in yilaalu. Yilaalu is an ageless melody, an everlasting story so old it is etched in the very earth itself. Yilaalu is the light from a cluster of stars so incomprehensibly far away they have ceased to exist. Yet still shine. Yilaalu is unfolding generations, passing on practices that, as we say, were born in the first sunrise.

Within yilaalu, the deep distance of past, I instinctively look in the other direction – to an equal point in the future the same distance away. Here, I see the same thing. Yilaalu yaluu. Yilaalu again. Yet here, yilaalu reveals an age where the physical world, to me at least, is unrecognisable. Where maybe the rivers of Yuwaalaraay cease to flow. Where people and language and custom are strange to me. Perhaps where my beloved Dharriwaa pulses with machination rather than birdsong. Stretching forward, yilaalu asks me to conceive of a time I know must come but will never live to understand.

Yuwaalaraay actuates such stretches and expanses of time, past and future on an infinite scale, by giving it the same word. Spoken, its sound encompasses what has always been and what is destined to come. Yilaalu – both a long time ago and a long time ahead. Yilaalu is past and future. It is the complexity of opposites sitting within the other, making a perfect, contradictory whole.

What can it mean for a place, or a person, or a community, to have a single word for that which seems so incredibly different? Well, perhaps it means you can be in two places at once, that time can and does fold in on itself, that language as well as giving explanation can also prompt question.

Yilaalu insists on an interaction with space. In this sense it is a geography, a philosophy, a pedagogy, a physics that contains a universe of meaning, in a few short shapes of lip, breath and tongue. When you live yilaalu, your world is shaped by things that are so great, they can only be explained through song, dance and artwork, through journeys and ceremony, and through narrative and imagery. Yilaalu not only asks you to speak but to listen, so that you might come to truly understand your place, your role, your value to the continuance of others. Living yilaalu means you are never alone. You are always connected and in relationship to that which has already happened and is certain to take place in the great connectedness – the lore of all living, once lived or to be lived things.

While yilaalu asks you to relate to the endless stretches and folds of time either side of this very moment, it also suggests that you think and engage with the now. It is yet another beautiful contradiction that surges from the banks of my homelands. Yilaalu voices one meaning while whispering another. Only if we stand firmly and confidently in the moment we occupy now can we come to feel the fullness of yilaalu's offering. Our old people, from right across the country speak about Tjurrkupa, The Dreaming, The Dreamtime, in Yuwaalaraay burruguu. And many say that within this great connectedness, within this time without time, the most crucial point is now. Yilaalu echoes this. It is only from the now that we can cast our gaze forward or back, into burruguu, into yilaalu, and fully comprehend our insignificance while caretaking the magnitude of the everywhen that surrounds us.

So, our now, this spectacular vantage point that raises us to yilaalu, is also an immeasurable point in the future, where the stories we tell are inconceivably distant, and our technology, our spaces and the way we interact are so foreign, that we ourselves are alien to the ones we descend from. We, the custodians of the now, are the very ones the singers of the first songs and speakers of the first words could never come to comprehend or know. We also at this very point in time are forgotten ancestors – faceless, nameless entities existent only in the dust that in turn comprises the universe herself. We are also our ancestors' wildest dreams. Songlines were made by us for them to follow and then pass on. Such is the power, the potency of people and language and culture and practice. Yilaalu once spoken scatters us throughout time, each cradling our own precious part of the now, allowing us to wrap in relation to others stretching into all parts of the always. Yilaalu ensures safe, happy journeys, whether they be back to the places we have come from, or onward to the places we must be.

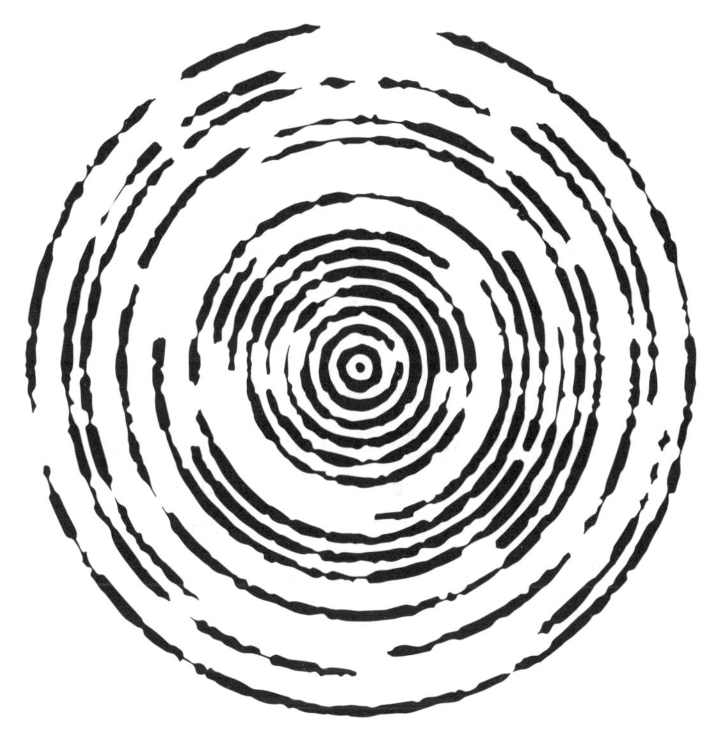

YUGARIE

Mykaela Saunders

DR MYKAELA SAUNDERS is a Koori/Goori and Lebanese writer and teacher, and the editor of *This All Come Back Now*, the Aurealis Award-winning, world-first anthology of blackfella speculative fiction. Mykaela won the 2022 David Unaipon Award for her manuscript *Always Will Be*. Her novel *Last Rites of Spring* was also shortlisted for the David Unaipon Award in 2020 and received a Next Chapter Fellowship in 2021. Mykaela has won prizes for short fiction, poetry, life writing and research, including the Elizabeth Jolley Short Story Prize and the Oodgeroo Noonuccal Indigenous Poetry Prize.

Yugarie is the Bundjalung word for pipi, the bivalve mollusc of the saltwater shores. Yugarie shells are cream or violet with pale grey or mauve striations, and they are shaped like butterflies when they are opened up flat. The interiors are smooth and purple. The meat that clings to the shell is the lightest pink.

I first learnt the word yugarie when my family moved up to the Tweed in the 1990s. We'd moved from our ancestral Dharug Country – Western Sydney – to the beautiful watery paradise of the Tweed. I fell in love with yugarie curry the first time I tasted it. One of our Elders had made a huge steaming pot of it for a NAIDOC lunch we had at the school, and it was served with fluffy white rice. The salty, chewy lumps of meat were so delicious in my mouth.

Up until then, I'd only ever eaten curried sausages. When I got older and yarned to other mob from different places, I realised that blackfellas everywhere have their own versions of curry and rice, but this staple delicacy has distinct regional and socioeconomic variations – mostly depending on which meats were cheap and readily available. Our people were using curry powders from the ration days, usually Keen's, to make all kinds of protein tastier. Some mob have traditions of curried roo, or curried crocodile, or store-bought chook. My family were always poor, so our version was curried sausages. But in the Tweed, where the waters are teeming with life, we were fast converts to yugarie curry.

I was taught how, where and when to gather yugarie: right between the tidelines, and preferably in the cooler months. We were only allowed to take the big ones so the little fellas would have a chance to grow up fat and fertile. We were taught this about all bushfood and seafood from a young age, along with other sustainable wisdoms such as: *always eat the fruit that is about to spoil first so that it doesn't go to waste.* These ways show why and how we've thrived in our Countries for so long.

Dig your feet into the sand and twist them down until you feel a yugarie, then grasp it with your toes and pass it up to your hand. Throw it back if it's too small, but put it in your pocket if it's nice and big. When you've taken your fill, put them in a bucket with clean salty water for a few hours so they spit out any sand they are holding. (It's a jarring feeling to crunch on a grain of sand while you're eating.) The shells stay open if the water remains at room temperature, and then it's easier to scoop the meat out. We'd chuck most of the empty shells back in the water, to break down and become sand eventually, but sometimes we'd make jewellery out of them.

I don't have a Bundjalung bloodline but I belong to a strong Bundjalung family due to generations of adoptions, both forced and welcomed. When I got older, and I learnt more about the history of my family and our community, I learnt that the yugarie was more than a good, free feed for us in the here and now. It's always been that, yes, but the yugarie also meant survival and identity for Tweed blackfellas, especially during the segregation period of government policy.

Ukerebagh Island is a huge mangrove island close to the mouth of the Tweed River. The Tweed is the most beautiful river in the world, my stepdad reckons, and not only that – it has nourished countless generations of Bundjalung people and other blackfellas, including South Sea Islanders, who became part of the Tweed Goori community. The name of the island, yugarie-bah, translates to 'place of the pipis' in English. Tweed Gooris were segregated onto this island from 1927, when it was officially declared an Aboriginal reserve. Two things made this place unique among most of the other Aboriginal reserves around this continent: first, it didn't have a resident manager, due to unsuitable living conditions like how mosquito-infested the place is; and second, the land here was unsustainable for farming because it was muddy and salinated. This helped to establish a bit of dependence on welfare rations – bland and bleached-out foodstuff like white flour, sugar and tea, which were poor substitutes for the nutritious food that Tweed Gooris were used to eating. But, being water people, they had the bounty of the river and the ocean at their disposal, and eating fresh seafood was the key to their survival on the island. They were able to gather yugaries to eat or to use as bait to catch bigger fish.

Our first Aboriginal senator, Neville Bonner, was born on Ukerebagh in 1922. Older people in my family were born on the island too, including one great-granny (Pa's mum), who looked after many babies who lived there along with her own. Pa's mum even had the surname of Yuke. I am unsure of whether the name relates to the pipi, but even if it is a happy coincidence, it has a powerful resonance for me within this history.

The reserve was a place of strict curfew – island residents had to be back on the island by 5:00 pm every day. But, because there was no resident manager, like most missions and reserves of the time, Tweed Gooris were able to sneak on and off the island whenever they wanted, using their intimate knowledge of the moon and tides, and using their skills in watercraft and navigation. They were able to visit family and friends who lived in other camps at Fingal and Tweed.

Even though it wasn't an ideal place to live, Tweed Gooris made the island their home, and so they were mostly devastated when the government closed the reserve in 1951 and forced them all off the island, though some families stayed until the late 1970s. Residents settled down in nearby communities at Fingal and South Tweed. Both places are right on the water, where yugaries and other river food can be found.

Through my Bundjalung family I am proud to be part of this history and to share this story – to show how our culture here in the Tweed revolves around helping each other, listening to the oldies and teaching the younger people, and knowing how to gather a good feed from the waters.

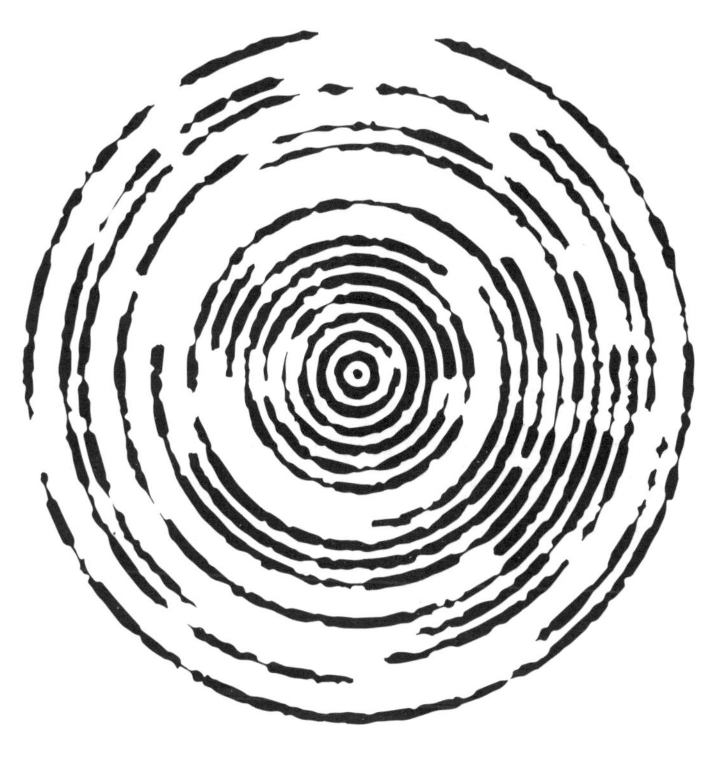

WUMARAGUNDAL

Cheryl Leavy

CHERYL LEAVY is from the Kooma Nation with connections to the Nguri people in western and central Queensland. Cheryl was the winner of the Oodgeroo Noonuccal Poetry Prize in 2022 and published her first picture book, *Yanga Mother*, in 2024.

I am from Kooma Country. I think in Kooma and I feel I must write in Kooma to affirm and sustain my Kooma belonging. I often make meaning with more certainty in Kooma than in English. For example, I call this continent Mudhunda, place of the song – three syllables carry all that we are.

The Kooma language is formally categorised as 'extinct' with limited resources documenting it. My formation as a Kooma person did not include a lot of language learning, but it did include emphatic instruction in the philosophy and practice of resistance, social justice and political rhetoric. I have returned to Kooma language as a poet, often writing pieces entirely in language or featuring key words in language. Writing is my preferred tool of resistance and liberation. My practice as a writer has prompted the discernment of new words in Kooma, usually from existing Kooma language and story.

The purpose of generating new words like Mudhunda is not merely to fill gaps in the history of our language, but to resist its colonisation and oppression, and to liberate my Kooma worldview.

Nothing has grieved me more than referring to the concept of Blak Sovereignty in the coloniser's tongue. This necessitates a new Kooma word: I offer wumaragundal. It is made up of two words: wumara is our word for woomera, a carved tool used to throw a spear, and gundal is our word for peace. Wumaragundal does not have the benefit of shared cultural memory to help it convey meaning. It must travel vast distances alone. Story will help it along, as it always has and always will.

★

To better understand wumaragundal – how both the word and concept came to be – I must tell you a story about Kguyalum, a story my uncle told me on our first trip out on Country together. I am grateful for his guidance in this telling of a story that others may also know to be true. Kguyalum was not a Kooma man but he is remembered and respected by my family as a warrior and diplomat of great intellect. In my family's telling, the story of Kguyalum is about the very creation of Mudhunda, our people's sovereignty over it and the observance of our law.

In the years before, Kguyalum travelled north to the place where Mudhunda was still connected to what is now known as Papua New Guinea. On these far northern lands many generations of warriors from near and far had resisted those who tried to cross the land bridge, making their way with bow and arrow. To protect his peoples Kguyalum struck a yam stick into the Earth, severing the land bridge. Kguyalum explained that the bow and arrow were not right for Mudhunda or its peoples, who had observed their responsibilities to this place for countless generations. Mudhunda was the land of the wumara, which Kguyalum declared as the eternal symbol of our law.

Enfolded within this simple telling of a big story is a great deal of cultural instruction, including the obligation to protect people and Country: right people for right Country, right cultural practice for right Country and right law for right Country.

★

The story of Kguyalum is perhaps one of the earliest accounts ever of First Nations peoples' collective wumaragundal over the continent and declaration that the observance of responsibility for Country is an assertion of rights.

In a Western legal and political sense, sovereignty is a supremacist concept. It is ongoing within the contemporary societies built by sovereigns – modern nation-states – who extract value from people and Country without meeting responsibility to the land or its peoples. Wumaragundal is more than mere sovereignty. It is not an assertion of supreme power over anyone or anything, but of shared cultural wisdom, connection and obligation. It is birthed into us by our Old People. We cannot be alienated from it. It cannot be contested. It is not determined, defined or limited by the democratic processes of any one generation.

Wumaragundal is sacred. Wumaragundal is practical. To declare Kooma wumaragundal is to proclaim spiritual and factual connection and obligation to Kooma Country and people. Like all of my people, I assert my wumaragundal and the cultural obligations that come with it by detailing my belonging.

At the frontier, around the time invaders first arrived on my Country, Kooma matriarch Kitty of Bollon was living on her Kooma land. Kitty birthed Emily, Emily birthed Annie, Annie birthed Beryl, Beryl birthed Patricia and Patricia birthed me. This is a statement of my wumaragundal. Yilu ngadju wumaragundalmi gurrgirri. This is my Blak sovereign strength. Yanga baga balgarra wumaragundalgu. As one of my Iningai sisters reminded me, mother is the root of wumaragundal. Yanga baga balgarra wandunbayalgu. Mother is the root of the law.

Ngaya guma. Yurdi ngadju bawurra. I am Kooma. My meat is red kangaroo. I am responsible for it and by meeting that responsibility I assert my wumaragundal. Collective practice of responsibility for Kooma Country is an assertion of our collective wumaragundal.

★

Wumaragundal is a matter of self-determination, nation to nation. I have been taught that it includes the right to the continued use of language. Writing in Kooma is an assertion and practice of Kooma wumaragundal. By constructing new words I am sustaining and practising my wumaragundalgu (Blak sovereign) right to my language as an individual. I believe Kooma people's collective wumaragundal over language is manifested if we decide that proposed words are accepted and enter common use.

Contemporary wumaragundal also incorporates rights to Country: to hold resource, property, water, intellectual and cultural rights, and to determine the application of resources that ensue from Country and cultural practice. Wumaragundal is the right and obligation to practise 'religious' beliefs, customs and traditions and to acquit our responsibilities as taught to us by our immediate ancestors.

Some of those responsibilities were taught to them in the same way. Some were observed on Country as part of both a spiritual and practical relationship between people and Country. Wumaragundal drives cultural continuation. It underpins our right to generate new culture – new ways of being and doing. We can and must develop contemporary cultural insights, in addition to sustaining customary knowledge and practice. It is what we have always done. It is how we have survived. It is how we have thrived. Wumaragundal wandhanja-wandhandja. Wumaragundal is everywhen.

⋆

Wumaragundal is a cultural practice taught to us by Bayama (Baiame) and Mandagada (Mundagutta, the Rainbow Serpent). The two creator ancestors connected us to the people and Country around us, forever obliging us to ceremony together at the places that they formed. On Kooma Country, we acknowledge their creation of the fish traps near the Murra Murra homestead, where we gathered seasonally with neighbouring peoples to honour gamu (water) and guyu (fish) and to honour each other by sharing resources.

Our creator ancestors forever connected us to them and each other by laying down Songlines, which acted like a treaty between nations and between the living and ancestral realms for countless generations. They taught us the power of ceremony, connecting Country, people and spirit through the languages of law, song and dance – carrying information about 'right way' for all time.

Yilu mudhunda wandhandja-wandhandja. This song Country is everywhen.

★

In my family, the telling of Kguyalum's story focuses on a deeper message – the desirability of peace and liberation. The yam stick symbolises our wumaragundal over our resources. By severing the land bridge with a yam stick Kguyalum gifted future generations the peaceful enjoyment of Country and its resources. The creation of the continent and the declaration that the practice of care for Country is fundamental to our rights are acts of land justice, a necessary precondition of peace.

In choosing the yam stick over the wumara to end conflict, Kguyalum elevated the wumara from its utilitarian status as a weapon. His declaration that it symbolises our law is a declaration of legal philosophy. In defining Mudhunda as a distinct place, with a distinct culture and law, Kguyalum established our wumaragundal as not just a belief or cultural practice, but a rule of law for this land and its peoples.

Ngawu! This is true and good.

★

Listen for the Voice of Sovereignty

Wumaragundal mardingu
Blak Sovereignty
Wangarra waalu wayal mudhun dhanduragu
The forever song of the stars

Gamu wumaragundalgu
Water is sovereign
You know this, it is your blood
Gamu waalu
Living water

Gamu nganagu ngulingga
Mandagada atoned water to Country – river, lakes, permanent waterhole
Water for all life

Gudumba wumaragundalgu
The Murray Cod is sovereign
    The gasping Murray is not your darling
    While millions of sovereign bellies meet the sun

Burdi wumaragundalgu
Fire is sovereign
Feel it on your tongue
'Burdi'

Yumburramban wumaragundalgu
Country is sovereign
Bagabaga nganangu dhungbilala
Gondwana, the rainforest from the
beginning of our time, burned

Can you not hear fire?
Yumbayayura burdi
Listen when fire speaks

Yarrgu wumaragundalgu
Air is sovereign
You know this, it is your breath

Bindjuyayura budharra dhaandu yaranguundu
Spit the ashes from your mouths
Roll back onto your bellies

Breathe
Bandjaya, sing!

★

This piece was written on Kooma, Yuggerah and Iningai Country, where Cheryl bore witness to the Seven Sisters creation story nestled deep in the cultural landscape they created. The seven stars are a small mark of her acknowledgement of both that story and its keepers.

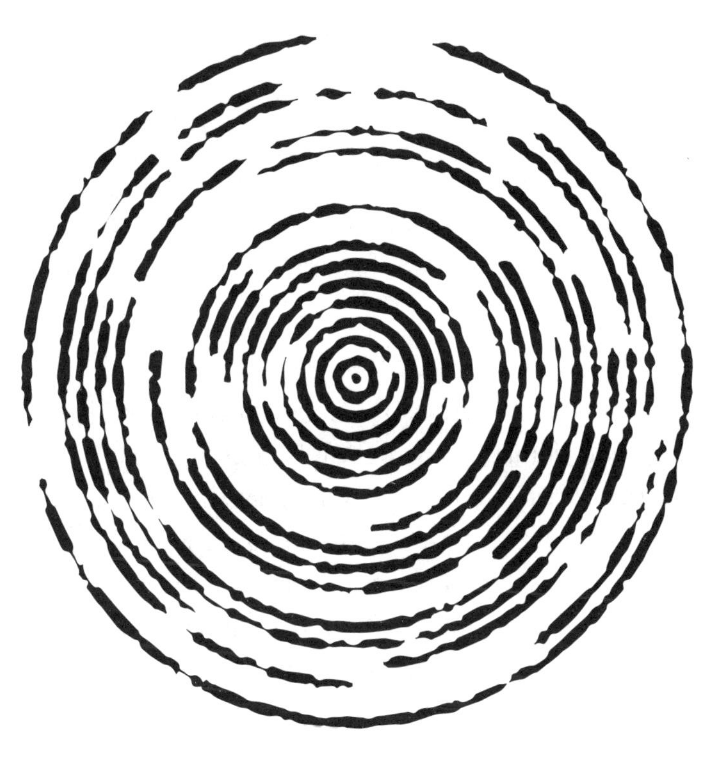

WALA

Taneshia Atkinson

TANESHIA ATKINSON is a Yorta Yorta and Bangerang woman living on Bundjalung Country. She is a freelance writer and an emerging poet and is passionate about exploring landscapes and healing through writing, as well as First Nations music. Taneshia's writing can be found in *Acclaim Magazine* and *Peppermint Magazine* among other publications, and is featured on Clothing The Gaps.

Wala (water) starts with the Murray River, which in Yorta Yorta language translates to Dungala. Dungala is wala. Dungala is our ancestor. Beyond my early childhood, I didn't grow up on my Country, which meant I was travelling back to see my family often. The long drives to Mooroopna were soaked in warmth, elation and excitement to see how much my little Aunties had grown, to reunite with my sisters and cousins, to feel the presence of our beautiful matriarchs and plant my feet on Country.

That feeling elevated whenever I reached the state border. I would, and still do, feel the energy of every cell in my body shift. But that wasn't because I was crossing into so-called Victoria. It was because I would drive over Dungala, which lines the boundary between Victoria and New South Wales. Seeing Dungala meant I was closer to my Country. Oftentimes I wished I could dive in and let Dungala carry me home or walk her banks until I reached Barmah.

It's widely known that colonisation for many communities eventuated in endangering our languages. Linguicide. I remember looking at an exemption certificate that stated my Uncle could leave the mission but doing so meant he wasn't allowed to speak his language, and I think of the generations after that were forced to speak English and silence their tongue. Each time I learn and understand our ancestral language, I feel the energy of our resistance in unity with, and parallel to, a sense of healing. I know I am not separate from my language. I'm learning language through an app, and it's important to acknowledge Aunty Sharon Atkinson, who I haven't yet had the privilege of meeting, for her work in reviving and sharing Yorta Yorta language, and for making me feel like I am returning to myself.

I used to dream of Dungala guiding me home and, through the knowing of wala, it did. Wala is in each space I embody and reminds me I am not a stranger here. Wala is home. Knowing wala means that water takes on a different, deeper meaning. Similar to water pooling, draining, flowing and flooding into crevices, the finding of wala seeps into every space of my life, deepening my existence and further grounding me. It is a relative.

it wasn't until
my language
returned to me
that water traversed from resource to ancestor
from water
        to
            wala
                                    personified
skin evaporating
        moisture dancing
returning to sky
speaking wisdom into clouds
to rain stories of Dreaming
guiding paths
        remembering
taking ache and pain to flow from my eyes
seeping into my bones
swallowing
carrying the beats of my heart to bleed another day
  another cycle
carrying life
floating, spilling
cleansing my spirit
remembering
        being
                    sentient

water is still
but wala reminds me that I am not a stranger here

water is quiet but I hear wala
hearing song and allowing me to taste moon
I feel wala
wala is a rhythm
in sky
in mouth
in hands
in coolamon
sitting on tongue as I orate

water is stagnant but
            wala is alive

wala surpasses time
it's not just always was
it's always will be
moving with you
moving in you
moving for you

the beginning
wala was here before the boats came
and prevailed after
when tear-stained faces needed washing
to cleanse

sustaining life
in cuppas
in gathering
in Dreaming.

—

I often think about this profound quote from Toni Morrison – '"Floods" is the word they use, but in fact it is not flooding; it is remembering. Remembering where it used to be. All water has a perfect memory and is forever trying to get back to where it was' – where she speaks about the act of straightening out the Mississippi River to make room for houses and liveable acreage and such, where occasionally the river would flood.

If I were to recreate this quote, I would say that 'wala has a perfect memory', which could also mean that all language has a perfect memory and is forever trying to get back to where it was, remembering where it used to be. Awakening.

Language is the antidote
wala has always been the antidote

with a perfect memory.

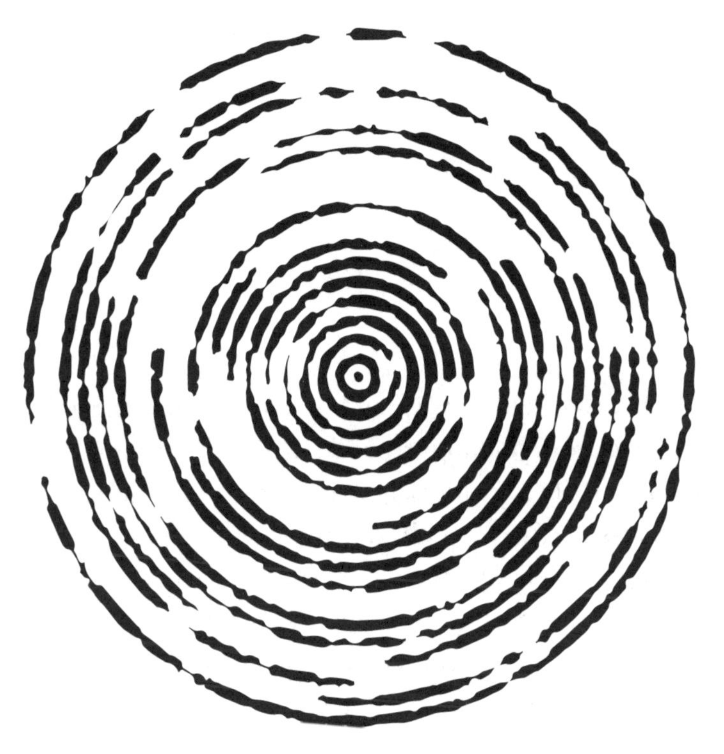

NGUNUNGGULA

Kirli Saunders

KIRLI SAUNDERS is a proud Gunai woman with ties to Yuin, Biripi, Gundungurra and Dharawal communities. She is a writer, multidisciplinary artist and consultant. Kirli has partnered with global organisations Google, Vogue, Fender, Qantas and Aesop to celebrate stories and cultivate change through visual art and writing. Her celebrated books include *Afloat*, *The Land Recalls You* and *Returning*, among others. Assisted by Creative Australia, she is writing a novel, a graphic novel and a poetry collection. You can also find her making music with her band Cooee, alongside Mark Harding.

With reverence and love for my Old People, and all Gundungurra People now and always. And for the land who raised us and gave us this word.

—

'Ngununggula'
Ngun-un-goo-lah

nun-un-goo-lah

Learn it slow
Speak it fast

'Ngununggula'

* nod *

Gundungurra Ngurra cascades and hikes. She's mountain ridges, caves, valleys, waterfalls and waterholes carved out by Creator Spirits. She's the language born at the ripples of the meetings of those landforms. Ngununggula is one of my favourite Gundungurra words.

It's the first one I felt tangibly roll and land in my mouth, as if the sounds of Country echoed in me like a birdcall bouncing off ancient stone. When I speak it, Ngununggula takes me home, to rambling rivers and the bush trails who birthed and raised me.

This land raised my parents too. Dad's settler family have lived in the area for the last century. Mum was brought here as a state ward, taken from her parents, and raised in various children's homes. We've got Gundungurra ties through my Pop's side and it was Pop's sister, a revered language teacher and local Elder, who first taught me this word. Aunty Velma Mulcahy OAM passed into the Dreaming in 2022, and I honour her and my Granny Amatto, who held this word for our family. Who refused to let it be silenced by missionaries, or the erasure laid out in policies and histories who denied our Language, our Lands and our Ways.

Ngununggula is resistance, and resilience in the highest form.

I understand it to mean 'to walk and work together' and also 'to belong'. Every time I utter Ngununggula, I feel that togetherness – a deep ancestral connection, an articulation of the bond between me, my Old People and the Country this word (and we) stems from.

For over 65,000 years, our languages and stories have been spoken, sung, danced or painted. It's only since colonisation that we've used written English to record them. Writing a word down doesn't necessarily capture the essence of that word. As an artist, I see Ngununggula as a shape drawn into the dirt – as our oldest shape, a circle.

The circle is ngurra – Country, camp, a nest, home. This shape is sacred geometry, the centre, the foundation of all life, the egg, the cell, the seasons, sun and moon, our stories – all innately rounded, returning, beginning, ending, starting again. It is all here, on this Country who grew me. Here, where I belong, a rounded, connected Ngununggula.

The circle is Mother, and with a concentric circle drawn inside: a womb. This shape depicts the relationality between mother and child. In Kinship, our little ones we call Bub, or Nan or Aunty, knowing she is a returned spirit, and also that she will become this matriarch – the outer circle, and so on.

This shape is past – a Mother (who was the child), present (both here now) and future (in that neither the Mother or child drawn initially here will remain, but continue into generations of our People). This concentric circle for me is about women handing down our knowledge, just as the women in my family have.

It's the teaching, sharing, belonging, the walking and working together – Ngununggula.

When I see a circle carved into stone, I see a star – grooved edges tapped or smoothed into rock by our Old People. They're part of a network, a celestial map with which to navigate the Sky Country. They tell us of creation, depicting ancient stories of place, seasons and Law. They're a portal to connect us to the continuum of time. As we look at the stars in the sky, we are looking at the past. And yet, when we read them with their carvings on Country, the same carvings our Ancestors made for us, we can see a way forward. This is Ngununggula.

When we dance or hold ceremonies, we do so in circles – earthly, sanded and stomped places for celebration and initiation. A circle to honour birth, growth, death, renewal, change. Always a circle – something to mark the continuation of our ways despite every harm from colonisation. Something melodic and embodied to say we were here, we are here, we will be here, always – Ngununggula.

For me, Ngununggula translates to more than a phrase. It's how we relate. It's in the way our Language has survived displacement. It's in every step of our bubbies as they sway on the sand, stomping and singing. It's in their cells, and the stories we tell them about the stars. It's who we are, and the women we come from. It's in the Land who gave us this word and who birthed us.

Ngununggula is a word I speak with reverence, and with love, for my Old People, and the Old ones yet to come, to whom I belong, and with whom I will walk and work, for all times.

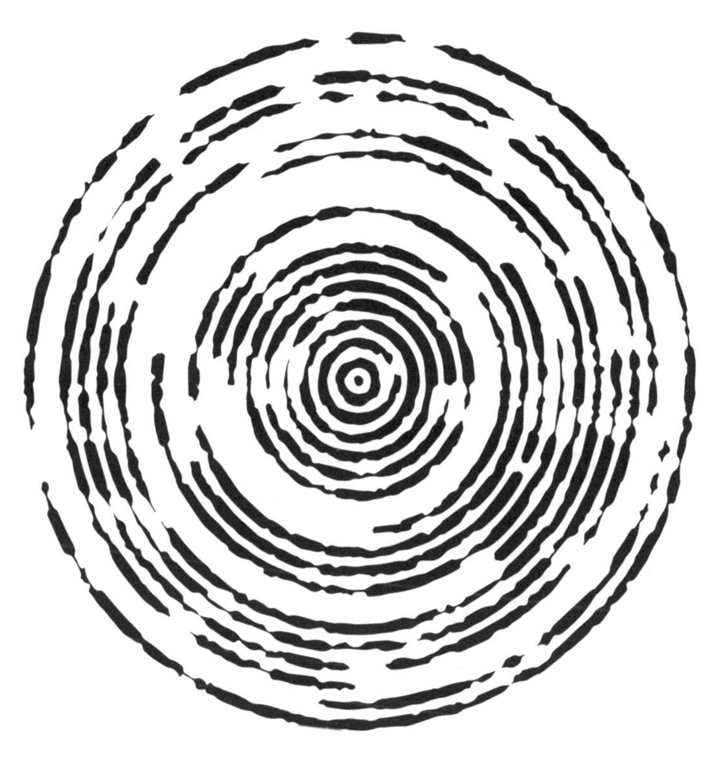

WIDJIWA

Alice Skye (Anderson)

ALICE SKYE (ANDERSON) is a Wergaia and Wemba Wemba person from Wotjobaluk Country in the Wimmera region. Known predominantly as a singer-songwriter, she has released two albums, *Friends with Feelings* and *I Feel Better But I Don't Feel Good*. Both explore feelings, healing and escapism. Alice learnt very young that when your surroundings are out of your control, there is comfort to be found in words, stories and songs. It is her hope to continue to foster that world of healing in whatever outlet that may be, including with the written word.

I miss the Country,
can barely stand still
I keep moving house because it's never home
I move my room around but it's never finished

I stand underneath the only gum-tree on the street
  where I live
Few doors down in the park for apartment-dwellers
Big, hundreds of years old I reckon
I circle around and hum Uncle Archie

'So bow your head old eucalypt and wattle tree …
… while the cities and the parks that they have planned
Look out of place because the spirit's in the land'

It's time I go home
Every time I'm back here I catch a cold,
maybe the city's leaving my body

Mum says it's the air
Sometimes I feel like leaving my body

There's a fallen red gum blocking the driveway
and I remember:
Bial, red gum
Buiga, to fall
We'll use it to stay warm

I stand on the back step to breathe
The way the air smells and the trees sound
The way the mountains feel like company –
big personality
We talk a little but not out loud

Spoke to my Aunty on the phone last night,
she apologised for talking too much
I hope she never stops

I'm in the far paddock and hear Mum chopping the
  wood
I think my dad lived and died near the mountains
Maybe I will too

Widjiwa, to return, to come home

Lyrics from Archie Roach, 'Native Born', from *Charcoal Lane*.

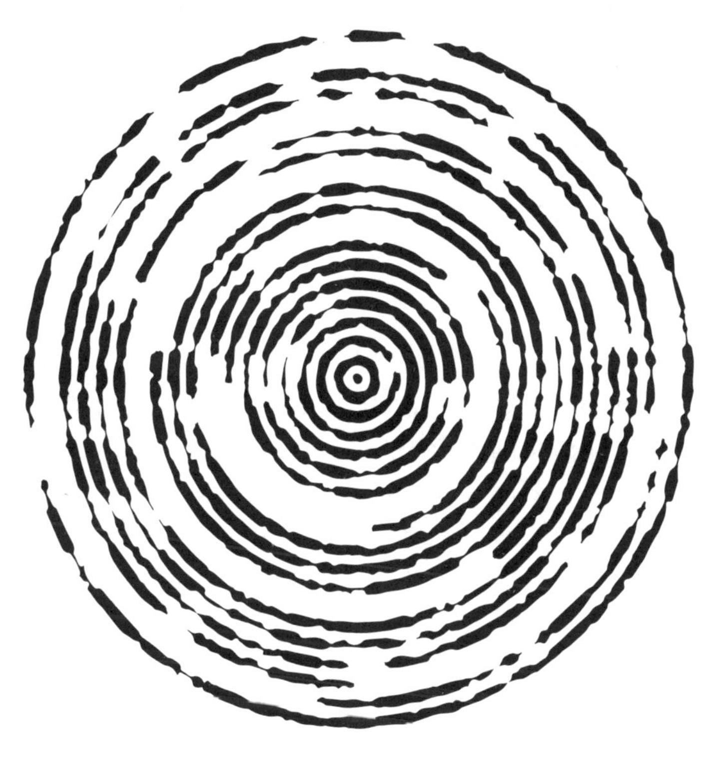

BUNI

Sasha Kutabah Sarago

SASHA KUTABAH SARAGO is a Wadjanbarra Yidinji, Jirrbal and African American writer, filmmaker and speaker. Her memoir *Gigorou: It's time to reclaim beauty, First Nations wisdom and womanhood* was published by Pantera Press. Sasha's TEDx talk 'The (De)colonising of Beauty' was selected as TED's 2021 Editor's Choice. Sasha has written and directed the documentaries *Too Pretty to Be Aboriginal* and *InsideOUT.*

The air is thick and caustic. My throat is chalky, like soot inside a chimney. I wear a mask along with others, finding it hard to breathe. Standing on the platform, trains play sliding doors while strangers search each other's eyes for hope – answers – when will this end?

The nights are no longer muggy, instead eerie as the smoke demon slithers through the crack of my door, determined to find me. My breathing is faint and nightmares replace dreams. What if this is my last breath and I fail to wake? Drowsy, smoke wrestles my eyes shut. Slumber erases the dread that lingers; will death become me? Until I rise to the same day as it was before.

Bloodshot auras infused with citrine flames curse the sky. They're calling it an apocalypse, and this is why I hate watching the news. My anxiety soars as I watch teardrops fall from helicopters into infernos. The smoke demon that visits me at night haunts the horizon. I watched a good Samaritan give a koala he rescued some water. The good deed is cut short when an awkward man wearing glasses stretches out his hand, but nobody wants to shake it.

A news anchor pans to families who have lost their homes and others who are desperately trying to save theirs. I watch despair etch their faces. And this is when I pray to the Creator to take pity on us while mobs far and wide gather for warrma (corroboree) – calling upon the Ancestors to bless us with jinda (rain).

While the mob dance up Country, others call for cool burns – the traditional way we care for Country, the way we've always done it, respecting the land and buni (fire).

You see, back in the jujaba (the beginning of time), not everyone had access to buni, only Walguy the taipan. Walguy was selfish and didn't share his buni with anyone else.

It didn't take long for the birds to grow tired of eating their food raw and freezing in the cold, to concoct a plan to steal buni away from Walguy. One by one, the Gurijala, the eaglehawk, Jiggiti Jiggiti, the willie wagtail, Gayambula, the white cockatoo, and Jawa Jawa, the magpie, tried to steal pieces of coal from Walguy, but to no avail. At last, Jawa Jawa called upon Bajinjila, the spangled drongo, to see if he would succeed. All the birds gathered to paint Bajinjila in black to disguise him, making his feathers smooth as silk to navigate the sky so Walguy wouldn't hear him.

Rising high in the air, Bajinjila dived into Walguy's camp and snatched the jiman (firestick) from him. Furious, Walguy chased Bajinjila, but he was too fast. And that is how Bajinjila stole buni from Walguy. That is how the birds were able to enjoy buni.

The buni story reminds me that buni does not belong to one but many.

How we use buni to care for the land is not one way but many.

Today, the First Peoples are the birds asking Walguy for buni to spark cool burns so that the mirrijin (medicine plants) grow back, the native animals return, and Country thrives as it always has long before the tall ships arrived. But like Walguy, they hoard their buni, using their jimans to spark big buni, too hot – too harsh for Country to bear.

Why are they bina guri? Why don't they listen? An Elder cries – he too is fed up from watching Walguy ignore the birds, Walguy's pride harming the land. Take heed. If you do not respect buni, it does not respect you. A lore my people had to learn, as I believe we all do.

As the wadjan bama, the rainforest people, the protection of buni was essential to our survival during the wet season. We had special gifts such as bagu (the fireboard) and jiman (the firestick). Bagu was made in the likeness of Chikka-bunnah, the buni spirit, a mystical being who appears as a shooting star by setting the night sky on fire with his jiman.

Chikka-bunnah was known to be a cheeky and malevolent spirit and feared by my people. Bagu and jiman were handled only by men, and one man in the tribe was responsible for keeping bagu and jiman safe and dry wherever our people travelled. Even the children were warned not to touch or play with bagu or jiman, or there would be consequence.

What if our respect for buni was like bagu and jiman? What if our fear of buni, like Chikka-bunnah, the buni spirit, and Walguy's selfishness was instead replaced by a relationship with buni to learn and listen to Country and the birds?

What if we let the cool burns restore what we have lost with only Country to regain?

All these stories told by my people remind me that our relationship with buni reflects our relationship with each other.

Buni is a reflection – a manifestation of ourselves.

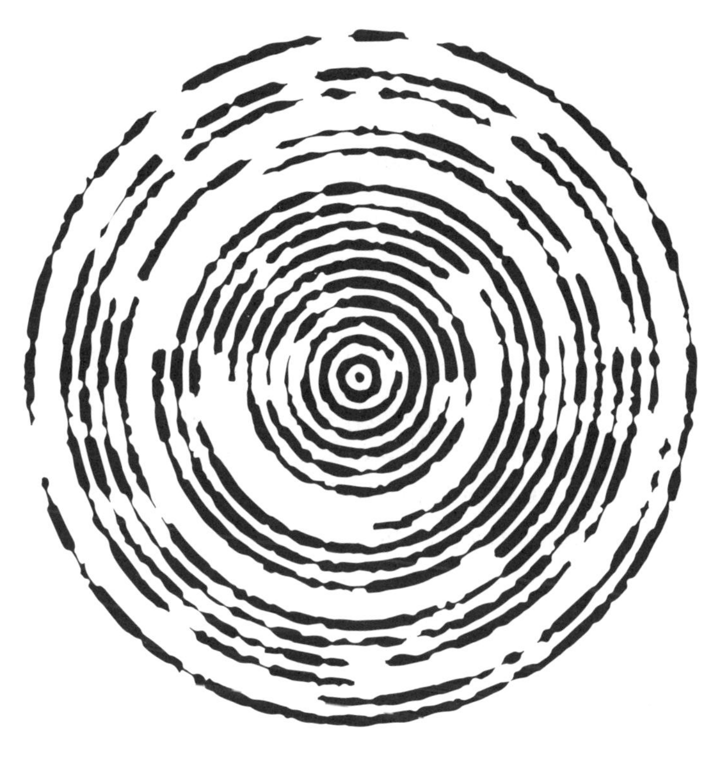

YARRAMAN

Kev Carmody

KEV CARMODY'S Indigenous heritage is Lama Lama (Cape York) and Bundjalung (northern New South Wales). He also has Celtic (Irish) heritage. He was born in Cairns and raised on the western Darling Downs in Queensland. He did labouring work until he was in his thirties, then went into higher education and then into music. His interests in life have been Indigenous studies and the ongoing evolution of culture and humanity. Nothing exists without a historical footprint.

Our old Aboriginal Grandmother and Grandfather used the word Yarraman when referring to a horse. Grandfather was a 'bush baby' from the Lama Lama area in Cape York and Grandmother was a Bundjalung woman from northern New South Wales. One of Grandfather's jobs was as a coach driver, while Granny was put on Wallumbilla Station to work as a domestic. Yarraman (horses) were a part of their daily existence.

Grandfather was in the Australian Imperial Force's (AIF) 5th Australian Light Horse Regiment and served in Palestine and Egypt in the First World War. He was a volunteer in the Second World War. He was promoted to Lance-Corporal and served at the Gallipoli Barracks in Enoggera in Brisbane because of his age. With Grandfather, Yarraman were essential to the AIF duties as a fighting force. Because of his traditional accents, when Grandfather pronounced the word

Yarraman, the 'rr's were sounded with a slight roll of the tongue – Ya*rrrr*aman.

The word Yarraman was heard widely in Cape York, and as kids we used it in the stock work we did as young boys in southern Queensland. During our stock work, horses were used by musterers and drovers. We used the Yarraman as draught horses, snigging logs for timber work, hauling drays, carrying pack saddles for our droving supplies, pulling our sulky to go to town, and as our working animals for mustering and droving.

Apparently the word Yarraman spread very quickly through our nations and communities along the east coast of Australia, reaching places such as the Yuggera Nation around Brisbane and the Lockyer Valley, and Wakka Wakka Country, as the area surrounding the South Burnett, Bunya Mountain and the Maidenwell region. Some analysts say the word Yarraman could have originated from the Dharug language from the Sydney district. 'Yira' meant teeth, or more specifically large teeth, which horses possess. So a man riding a horse then suddenly became Yarraman in our First Nations vocabulary.

From our family's standpoint, it was part of our oral history, passed down from our grandparents to us. The Yarraman played a vital role in our existence as First Nations people, and the word Yarraman is still commonly used today as our people reclaim their languages.

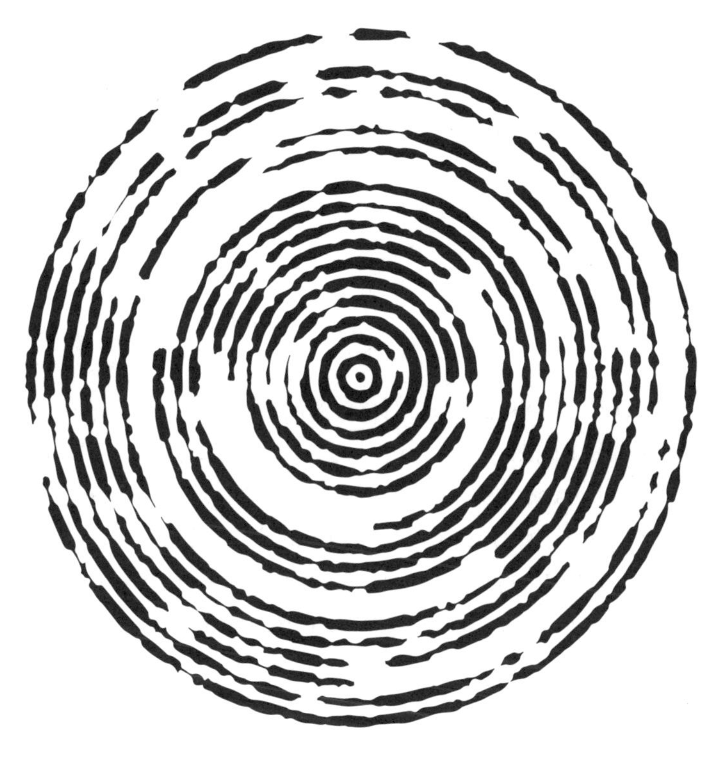

SPEAKING NUKUNU WARRALA

Jared Thomas

DR JARED THOMAS is a Nukunu person of the Southern Flinders Ranges and a research fellow (Aboriginal and Torres Strait Islander Material Culture) at the South Australian Museum and the University of South Australia. Jared is the highly regarded author of critically acclaimed books for children and young adults.

There were a lot of things that weighed against me learning Nukunu warrala (language).

Firstly, stopping people from speaking language was one of the ways Australian governments took control of Aboriginal land. The colonisation of my South Australian Nukunu and Ngadjuri family was swift and brutal. When I was in my twenties, I was walking down the street of Port Germein and my Aunties told me that my great-grandfather, Alexander Thomas, used to insist on speaking language, and his family would growl him. They did this because in some places your kids were taken from you if you were teaching them language.

About the same time, I was told the story of how, as an old man, my great-uncle Gilbert Bramfield was in a Port Pirie bar speaking his language and one of his relatives warned him not to. 'Why not? They speak their own warrala,' he protested.

Uncle Gilbert passed away in 1974, two years before I was born. During his life he worked with linguist Luise A Hercus to ensure the Nukunu language was recorded. This work resulted in the resource *A Nukunu Dictionary* by Luise A Hercus, published by the Australian Institute of Aboriginal and Torres Strait Islander Studies in 1992. The recordings of Uncle Gilbert speaking language have also contributed to the Nukunu language resources made available by the University of Adelaide's Mobile Language Team. However, the language continues to be a threatened one.

The words I remember from when I was little are tjina, murra, kudna, wapma, warkala and abmiwara. Some of these words are still spoken in everyday language by family members, even those who don't really have a desire to learn Nukunu language. The words are just so ingrained.

Wapma, snake, is our totem and he can be seen in Abmiwara, the Milky Way. I feel that this word lived on in Nukunu memory due to wapma's dominance in Nukunu identity.

Dad also has WOK tattooed on his left fingers, standing for warkala, the crow, one of the Nukunu totems, and a name shared by uncles before him.

Murra and thitna are your hands and feet, and kumpu and kutna are what you do when you go to the toilet. Murras and thitna are also words that are shared across many Aboriginal languages, which probably assisted their longevity when Nukunu people weren't actively trying to maintain and develop language.

I always thought that speaking Aboriginal language was a cool thing. My Aunty Kathy, my mum's sister, would speak language that was not handed down through her Aboriginal family, but spoken by her friends and picked up by her. Kuga was one of the funny words I learnt from Aunty Kathy as a kid. We used to say that someone's got kuga when their underwear or bathers are climbing up their murntu, their backside. Kuga is a Pitjantjatjara word that means 'meat'. So, when you're seeing someone's murntu hanging out of their underwear or bathers you're saying, 'I can see your meat.'

The word deadly is commonly used among Aboriginal and Torres Strait Islander people across the country to express that something or someone is really good. The word solid is used in a similar way, and I remember solid being used more as an exclamation than deadly until I was in my twenties. Aboriginal people picked up the use of the word deadly as an expression from the Irish, which tells us about the relationships some Aboriginal people had with early Irish settlers.

Fortunately, I grew up and worked in an environment where speaking Aboriginal language was practised and valued by those around me, and it made me want to learn more of my own people's language.

Throughout the 1990s Hercus's *A Nukunu Dictionary* started being shared with our community. I began looking at words in the dictionary around then and I would check in with relatives and friends from neighbouring language groups, the Adnyamathanha, Barngarla, Narrunga, Ngadjuri and Kaurna, to help with the pronunciation of Nukunu words, as their languages are very similar.

It wasn't until about ten years ago that I first heard the recordings of my great-uncle Gilbert speaking Nukunu language. The recordings of Uncle Gilbert by Luise Hercus were conducted between 1960 and 1971, and the 1960 recording field notes indicated that they were conducted at Uncle Gilbert's camp near Port Augusta, with other recordings occurring at Port Germein. Uncle Gilbert's voice was a bit gruff but he spoke very good English, and he took great care in pronouncing and explaining the meaning of Nukunu words and their connection to others. Luise spoke with a very refined accent, synonymous with the period, and what was most apparent was the rapport between Uncle Gilbert and Luise.

I found listening to Uncle Gilbert speak language and gaining further insight into his life through the recordings a very emotional experience. I am pleased that my cousin Anil Samy utilised these recordings with the Mobile Language Team at the University of Adelaide to create audio word lists for people wanting to learn Nukunu language.

My daughters have a strong interest in Nukunu language. My daughter Delilah recently made word lists for her baby sister. My older daughter Tilly has written several songs that feature Nukunu language that have been played on Triple J Radio. Her song 'Ngana Nyunyi', meaning 'What's that?', is about learning Nukunu language based on a game we used to play, where I would ask Ngana Nyunyi and my girls would name things in Nukunu language. Ngayi Yurlku Nhiina means 'I love you' and it was quite incredible to hear this most common phrase sung by my daughter in Nukunu language on national radio.

Naming places on Nukunu Country and speaking Nukunu language is for me a way to honour my Nukunu ancestors, a way of keeping their memory alive. It brings me much satisfaction to name places that are commonly known by their English names in Nukunu language. Our language also tells us about the types of animals or plants that are important to and dominant in a particular area and the Dreaming stories and ancestors that are connected to them.

A way that I work to ensure the continuity of our language is to include Nukunu language in the young adult and children's fiction that I write. Other family members provide workshops for school children where they teach them Nukunu language as part of learning about Nukunu culture.

My hope is that in the future there's many more fluent Nukunu language speakers. For the moment, I am delighted by the young people in our family learning and speaking their language and understanding the power of it.

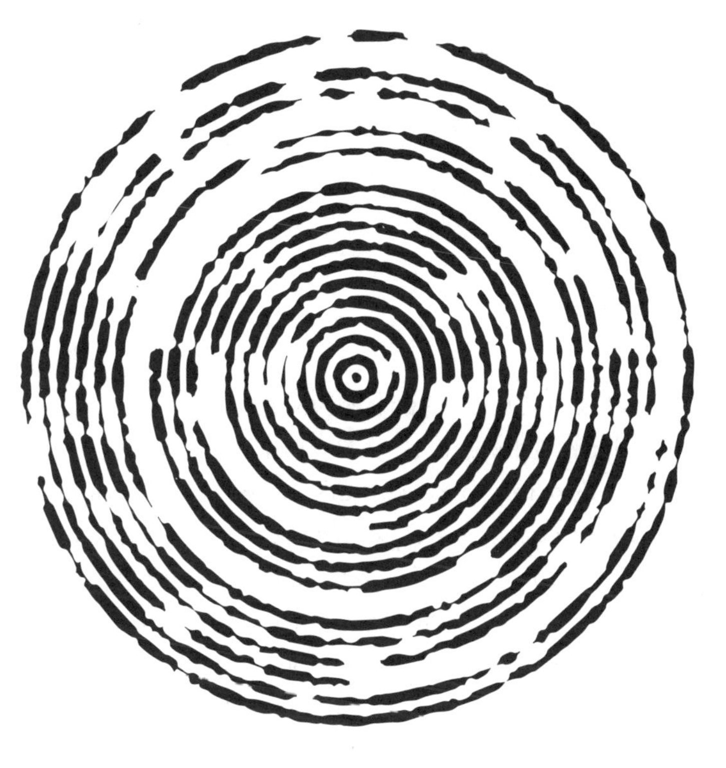

BILYA – BILA – BEELIAR

Claire G Coleman

CLAIRE G COLEMAN is a Noongar woman whose family have belonged to the south coast of Western Australia since long before history started being recorded. She writes fiction, essays, poetry and art criticism while either living in Naarm (Melbourne) or on the road. Her first novel, *Terra Nullius*, won the 2016 black&write! Indigenous Writing Fellowship. She has published two more novels, *The Old Lie* and *Enclave*, and a non-fiction book, *Lies, Damned Lies*, which unpacks the effects of the history of Australia's colonisation.

I live for wild natural water, for rivers and streams, the ocean they all, in the end, flow into, choosing my homes, when I have the opportunity of choice, for their proximity to waterways, choosing waterways to camp near when I travel. I cannot use a bridge, cross a river, on foot without stopping to stare at the water and for a moment at least, and every time, I lose myself. My hobby, when I have time, is fishing, taking time by the river bank to relax and feel and, sometimes, just be.

If you took water from me forever, if I was to live in the desert and never return to the river bank (although I do love the desert in its own way), I would lose myself, I would no longer be me, for I am water, and belong near water. If there is one thing I have written about more than any other – except perhaps colonisation – it's water, my love for it, my desire to be near it, my connection to it as family. When I die I will be cremated and my ashes returned to water on my Country, for in water on my Country is where I know, in the depths of me, I belong.

And that is what Bilya is – evidence of that connection to our waterways our Country and our family, of how my Noongar family are connected to the waterways, how the rivers of our Country are our mothers, how rivers and streams define us, tell us who we are. How we know where we are, how we know where we belong. We mapped our Country by waterholes and by Bilya.

One meaning belonging to the word Bilya, in my ancestral language – the language I barely know any words of, the language named Noongar after my ancestors' word for man – is river, or stream. Our rivers and streams are not like rivers in other places, they tend to be formed in estuaries. When they are open to the sea, cutting though sand dunes, to the wardan, more often than not they are closed at the mouth, blocked by walls of sand deposited by the surf faster than the flow of the river can push out. It doesn't rain enough on my Country to make the rivers flow – they are so shallow we once used them, and still do, as our walking paths.

Many of our Bilya end at deep tannic lakes, separated from the ocean by dams of sand, but not before the salt water had entered, the water becoming saltier as the sun and hot, dry air boils away the water. Also on Noongar Country, and on other parts of Boodjar, there are rivers that stay open, though they are estuarine for much of their length. But my Boodjar, in the south, has no mighty rivers, yet all our rivers are sacred.

And Bilya is more.

The Bilya is our mother, our love, our breath – she gives us our life, the river is who we are and we are children of the river. Our homes are the coasts where the rivers meet the sea, our homes are the river and its banks all the way to the source, each family is connected to a waterway, our homeland is the catchment of that water. It joins us to Country, it takes us home.

Bilya is also, rather adorably, our Noongar word for belly button, which ties us to our mothers (and through our mothers to our Boodjar). The umbilical cord, which gave us sustenance before birth, adjoins us there; the rivers flow to the sea but never make it and the navel is a closed connection – we are separated from our mother lastly at the Bilya. This is a fitting metaphor, we were connected to our mother at the Bilya, as Bilya connects us to the ocean. You don't need to dive in and imagine for long to know how appropriate this is – you just have to feel it. The water is our mother.

The Bilya is the everywhen, it flows like time – we can flow with it, into our future, from our ancestral past, and back again and again from mother to mother to mother. We can trace time also by the line of our ancestors, the lines of our mothers go back forever. It is by connection, and life, we are reminded of who we are and where we come from – we are connected to our mother country, eternally in the everywhen, through the Bilya.

The bones of my ancestors are forever on my Country, my ancestors are the bones of Country. There are bones too in Country that the wadjela planted there, hoping from our bones a great nation would grow. There are bones in Country that are swept out of the gullies into the Bilya when it rains, joining the other bones, and the bones of Country in the life of Country. And when my ashes are returned to the water on my Country I will be there, in mother wardan, when the mouth of the Bilya opens again, when the saltwater joins the fresh, when my ashes join the bones of my ancestors and the bones of my Country.

I can become one with my Country, reborn through the Bilya; reborn into the eternal everywhen. And then forever I will live by the Bilya, for in the everywhen the Bilya is eternal.

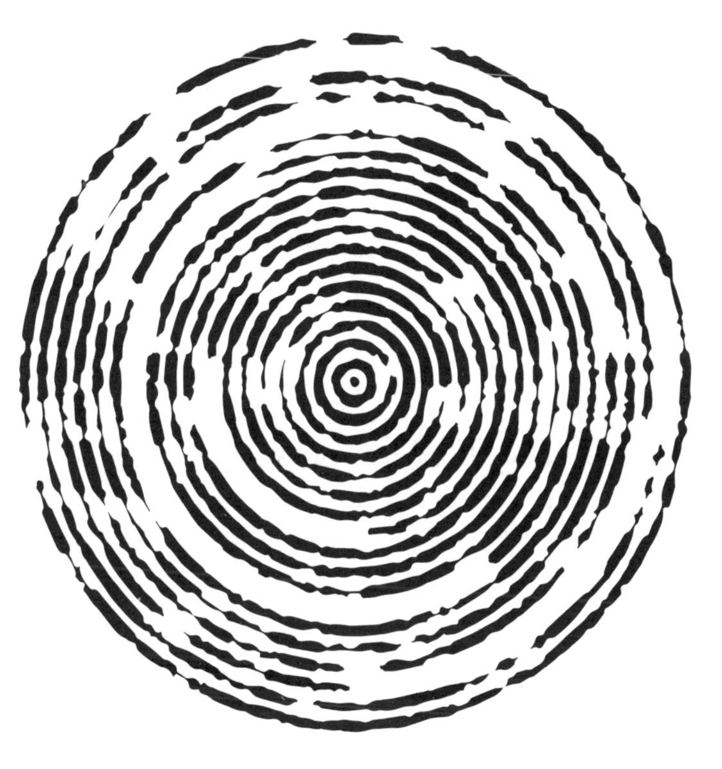

NGULLINGAH JUGUN

Bronwyn Bancroft

DR BRONWYN BANCROFT is a Bundjalung woman and artist. Bronwyn's career has included both national and international exhibitions. Her contribution to Indigenous literature has been immense, including the publication of forty-five books. Bronwyn has a Diploma of Visual Arts, two Masters degrees and a Doctor of Philosophy from the University of Sydney. Bronwyn is a volunteer and advocate for equality and contributes her extensive expertise to a number of community organisations, including AIME, Boomalli Aboriginal Artists Co-operative and The Returning.

As a young girl growing up in a small country town, the memories of going to my grandmother's Country for school holidays are some of the most vivid images etched into my brain. The freedom of being immersed in creek games as the hours slipped by and our crinkled skin emerged from water saturation. The animals that surrounded our grandmother and grandfather's place were plentiful with platypus, catfish, turtles and eels, as well as goannas, which were enormous.

I felt safe there with all my family around me. I don't believe my old people are ghosts – I believe and feel their strength as they stand beside me. We are them and they are us. It seems like a long time ago, but I can still sense the water on my skin and the sweet smell of a freshwater creek.

I have been requested to write about a word or phrase in Bundjalung that is important to me. I have chosen Ngullingah Jugun, Our Country.

Our people of the Djanbun clan were massacred at Nogrigar Creek on our traditional Country in 1840. We are the survivors of our great-great-great-grandmother, Pemau. With all the ongoing discussions that abound in this country, named Australia, there is one essential truth that no-one should fail to understand: this country was taken by force by many settlers whose aim was to steal land that didn't belong to them, and to decimate the First Peoples who have been the custodians of Country, in our nations, in our clans and in our families.

My heart breaks every time I hear another person say that this Country was not stolen and that it was colonised by superior people. I disagree as our people were murdered and no justice was accounted for. Many people are wilfully ignorant of the historical atrocities inflicted on Aboriginal and Torres Strait Islander people. The Frontier Wars, including many massacres and acts of manslaughter, were sometimes documented in settler journals, although there were many that were not recorded.

This has left a sadness that may never leave my heart but has acted as a pivotal catalyst for change and truth-telling.

I am uninterested in having to educate ignorant people – there is just no reason for ignoring the truths about the longest-enduring People on the planet. Do not disregard our AI – Aboriginal Intelligence – as survival is imprinted in our DNA.

It is essential that our society disregards the racist rhetoric that has been perpetuated in our schools, other places of learning and the wider culture of this continent. Our history and a deeper and truthful understanding of our shared existence together is the foundation for a healthy partnership with our Mother Earth.

I have spent the majority of my adult life highlighting the disparity and inequality that exists, and existed historically, for our family and the wider community. Ignorance is not a reason to deny justice.

I have been a custodian for the last twenty-nine years of some land that was purchased by my Uncle Pat Bancroft. I have held that place for family and lived there when my children were young, to take them back to Country. We had no electricity or much of anything except each other and the land, and we would travel with Uncle Pat to learn sites of significance for our family.

I always say I have continued to maintain a fingerprint in our Country. Keeping this place in our traditional area has not been easy while raising three children as an artist and single mother, but the whispers from my ancestors infiltrated my being and I took on the responsibility. My Uncle Pat died in 2015, the last of our dad's family, and with his death we lost not only his wisdom but also a link of lived experience and knowledge about our Country.

All the men in our family were enlisted to serve in the armed forces even though they were not recognised as citizens of Australia. They thought they would be treated as equals when they returned from defending this country but that was not to be. I asked my dad, Bill Bancroft, why he went to war and his response was, 'It's my country too, Bronwyn!'

As an artist and a writer, I have written and painted stories over many decades about Ngullingah Jugun, our family connections and our history in an attempt to highlight the endurance and tenacity of my family. This is not a revelatory story for our mobs, but it is for an external audience of those outside our culture.

As with any colonised country, the attempted genocide and abuse of Aboriginal and Torres Strait Islander people as slaves, forcing them to assist in building the colony, along with taking children from their families and dispersing clans, taking over land and implementing a framework of assimilation, was all part of a strategic plan. This plan was readily enforced by many who were 'gifted' large tracts of land to build their new lives, while they left our social cohesion, family networks and cultural ties to Country in tatters.

We are healing from devastating losses and rebuilding our lives that are defined by our love for each other and respect for our families and communities. We are still treated with disregard and contempt by people who have benefited from stolen land, stolen children, stolen wealth and wages. This country is known as 'Incarceration Nation' due to the continual locking up of our people since the establishment of the colony.

I wrote these words in 2023 and I believe it's time for the truth of this country's unsettling past to be brought out into the light. We all need to heal. Having the colonisers' descendants speak about their families' involvement in the Frontier Wars is just the beginning, but it is an essential step forward in starting a new chapter of living in reciprocity and kindness. In Ngullingah Jugun.

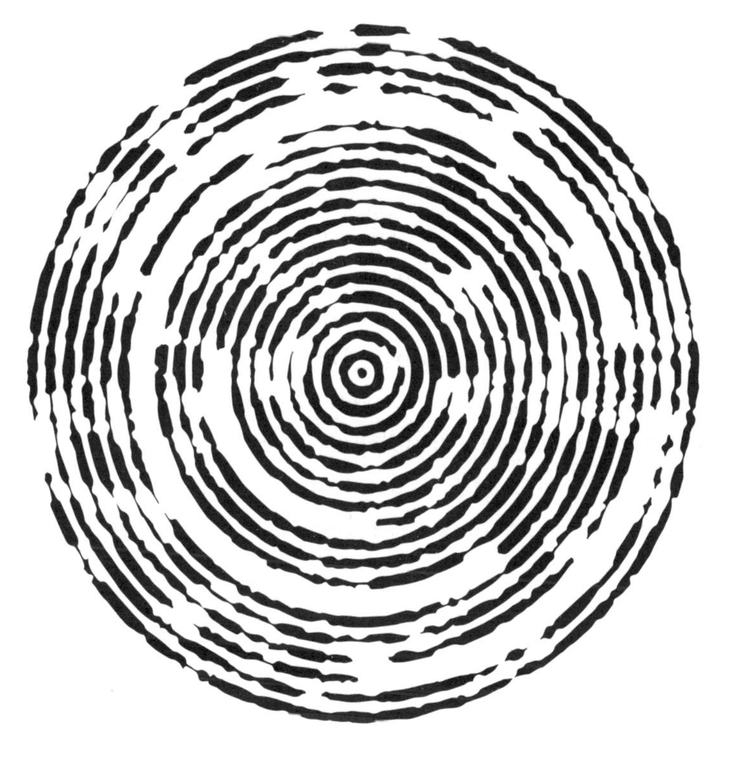

DUMULARRA

Judy Watson & Otis Carmichael

JUDY WATSON was born in Mundubbera, Queensland. Her Aboriginal matrilineal family is from Waanyi Country in north-west Queensland. Judy works across painting, printmaking, drawing, sculpture and video. Her work is included in several significant Australian and international collections. Judy is an Adjunct Professor at Griffith University, and in 2018 she was awarded an Honorary Doctorate of Art History by the University of Queensland.

OTIS CARMICHAEL is a Waanyi man born on Larrakia Country in Darwin. Having studied information technology, he now works in the Indigenous language research space, following his passion for the collaboration between First Nations languages and technology, and their cultural impact. He expresses himself through cooking and writing, which he uses to connect to his ancestry and identity.

Dumularra: current of water, flowing water (Waanyi language). My grandmother's Country is Waanyi Country in north-west Queensland, cut by the Northern Territory border. We are known as running water people. Boodjamulla (Lawn Hill Gorge) is Mumbaleeya (Rainbow Serpent Country) where the ancestral snake carved out the gorges and shaped the land.

Our mountains are the Constance Range, the blue-green subterranean body of water where Boodjamulla resides is Duwadarri. Lawn Hill Creek, Gregory River and the O'Shannassy River are some that run through here. This is ancient water that the dinosaurs were drinking. It emerges through fissures in the limestone from deep beneath the surface of the Barkly Tableland.

Wanami is our word for water. Other Waanyi water words are: winjaraba (water poured on), marrarrabada (water women), bilikija (swim), yanja (big waterhole), jiwil (spring), jala-wanyi (freshwater).

I think through water as a medium. When I'm swimming, washing clothes, soaking materials, pouring and pooling washes of liquid paint onto my canvases and paper in the studio, water acts as my conduit to a higher state.

Water is delicious to swim through, submerge in and float upon. Water connects me to fluent thinking and imaginative ideas. Water is a weapon. During the Frontier Wars our waterholes were deliberately poisoned. Massacres of our people often occurred near water. Now poison is seeping from agricultural run-off, mine tailings and fracking. Contaminants are leaching into our river systems.

Some long-haul mining is cracking through riverbeds and forcing precious water to drain away. The springs in the flat plains of the Gulf that were mapped during early colonisation are now inactive. Springs that I observed at Louie Creek in 1990 are no longer bubbling up. Elder Aunty Eunice O'Keefe thought they may have been drained by the nearby mining operations.

Images of the rainbow on rock art in our Country allude to the Rainbow Serpent. My grandmother asked her mother about the springs they'd visited. Her mother told her, 'The rainbow dried it up.' 'Boodjamulla keeps the deep gorge holes full of water to keep his body wet; if he ever leaves, the water will dry up,' said Uncle Arthur Peterson.

Water is our wellspring, our lifeblood. Confluences, sources, undercurrents – water is the medium that connects us to this place and to each other. Water has a memory that trickles and pools and follows the topography of djamba (ground) – it is the hidden jewel that feeds the Country. When I am immersed in water, I feel connected and alive.

—

Ngawu Otis, jarribirri Waanyi burrurri. My name is Otis, son of Judy, grandson of Joyce, great-grandson of Grace. I'm a proud Waanyi man, dumularra runs in my veins.

Dumularra is always referred to as its own entity, an entity represented by flowing water. But more intuitively it is the force of water. Dumularra has the power to destroy, carving deep scything gorges through the arid rock of Boodjamulla, north-west Queensland, or tearing out the shallow roots of the palm trees that follow its course, only to cast them aside. But of course, dumularra brings life, sparkling clear healing waters that bubble up through limestone aquifers and drawing in all manner of animalia – snapping turtles, people, red kangaroos.

Dumularra is difficult to pin down. How do you pick up dumularra? It is flowing water, it is running water, it is flooding water. The instant that you isolate it, identify it, you have lost it – the force resists capture. This wanami is potential taking space, taking shape. Swelling and receding through the seasons but never losing its reserved coolness, refusing to let the heat penetrate its surface.

Dumularra is a teacher for me. As it surges its way above the banks that hold it, I am reminded of my false ideas of safety. Particularly, that wooden houses and concrete drains will protect me from fierce waters. But dumularra is rising and nothing is going to stop it. The view of the creek bed that has been changed completely over the course of another momentous wet season, debris and organic litter swept clean by dumularra, a reminder not to grow too attached to the way of things. We are Waanyi, running water people. We ripple and shift as we flow.

Yimbirra nyulu bikalii, dumularraa. Janybijbi
nyulu, janybijbi, jalwaa dumularraa.
The floodwaters carried the stuff along with it.
It discarded it along the way, the strong current did.

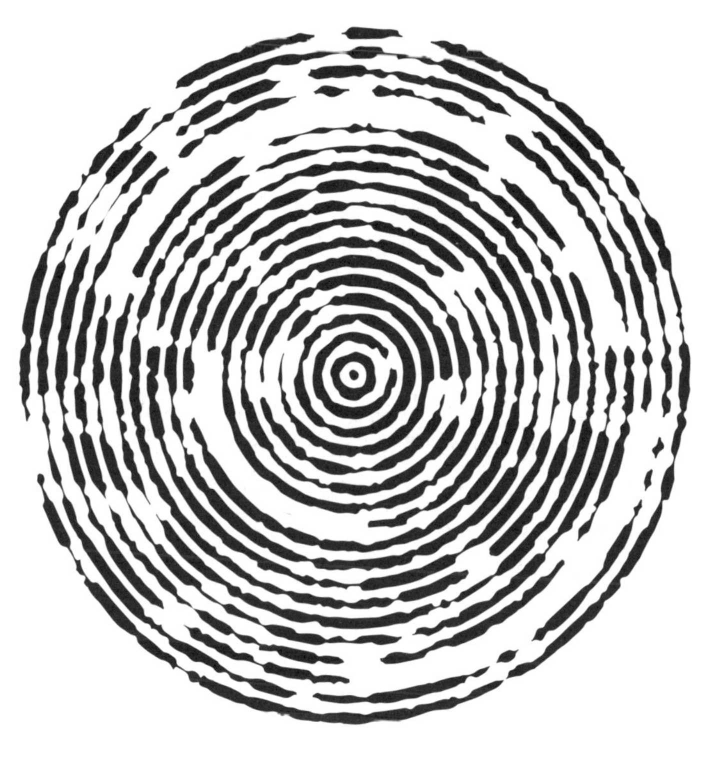

DECOLONISING THE SHELF

Tara June Winch

TARA JUNE WINCH is an Australian (Wiradjuri) writer based in France. Her first novel, *Swallow the Air*, was critically acclaimed and a tenth-anniversary edition was published in 2016. She was previously mentored by Nobel Prize winner Wole Soyinka as part of the Rolex Mentor and Protégé Arts Initiative. Her short story collection *After the Carnage* was published in 2016, also to critical acclaim. Her latest novel, *The Yield*, was published in 2019 and won the 2020 Miles Franklin Literary Award among other prizes, and has been translated widely. She is working in film and writing her fourth book.

Back in 2018, I was speaking at the Canberra Writers Festival when I was asked a question by a woman during the audience Q&A. The woman was baffled – she wanted to know why she was only now discovering so many First Nations writers. She wanted to know, in her words, 'Why the explosion, what has changed?'

I answered intuitively, a little hurried for time. I said that, contrary to any sense of great change or explosion, we are a culture that has survived by storytelling; we have a long history of writing, and we've continued to write and publish. It wasn't us who changed, I said, it was her. The collective readers of Australia had finally recognised their national identity crisis and responded in turn.

I don't know if this was entirely correct. I've noticed the times as much as she has. I've realised that readers are embracing our stories as their own. In the past few years, I've seen anthologies of First Nations' writing published, the presence of our books in top-ten and prize listings – and, of course, I've noticed festival audiences for events featuring First Nations writers increase in numbers, in openness and in the questions they ask.

I thought about this woman later and wondered: had I been paying attention fully? Had I been fully aware of that great canon so many people never knew or still don't know, the books that us contemporary First Nations writers carry on our backs – just as we carry the past, and our ancestors' stories too.

The United Nations International Year of Indigenous Languages was acknowledged in 2019, a year that celebrated and promoted protecting the 2,680 native languages around the world that were – and still are – in danger of being lost. Our languages are essential to our unique cultural and historical identities and traditions, and to navigating our future autonomy, human-rights protection, peace-building environmental care, reconciliation and reparation, and sustainable development.

Before the colonisation of Australia, 600 language groups comprised the oldest surviving civilisation on Earth. Inseparable from these languages are their stories: they decode not only the rules of linguistic order, but also the skies and seas and land masses and family relations and how the world itself came to be. Locked in languages are hundreds of physical places that a speaker may never even visit. Languages themselves are navigation manuals for living in this part of the world.

Back then, in 2019, with around sixty surviving languages and increasing awareness of language importance as a living artefact, there was already a renaissance in Indigenous language reclamation and learning in Australia. And this is ongoing as school programs are being developed to support maintaining and using Indigenous languages, and some publishing houses release books written in Indigenous languages. If we know that culturally and linguistically responsive pedagogy contributes to academic success and sound mental health, do we also now grasp the ways our stories contribute to a more understanding and inclusive society?

I think we are beginning to.

We need to break the default of our reading habits to hear stories about ourselves as Australians. We are not only blue yonder and hard yakka; life is lived beyond the nuclear homestead. We are migrant and refugee, gay and trans, city dwelling and still incarcerated. We are millions of voices – and we are, in particular, the original Aboriginal and Torres Strait Islander languages of this continent. We are tongues before David Unaipon wrote *Hungarrda* in 1927 and *Legendary Tales of the Australian Aborigines* thereafter. We are stories that not only run across the entire country, but have appeared in many other cultures, just as the story of the Seven Sisters is alive in the Pleiades constellation of Taurus on this side of the world as much as it was alive in ancient

Greek mythology. We are contemporary storylines that cross old missions, towns and cities too, now narrating for us that terrible inheritance with as much literary heft as the best stories have.

On the whole, First Nations have been publishing in assimilated language in postcolonial Australia. Our writers were required to use that vehicle of expression to transmit their experience. But increasingly we can break – and have already been breaking – the mould of English with new works published bilingually. These seem like radical acts, yet with so many of our people speaking English as a second, third, fourth or fifth language in this country, perhaps it's actually a startlingly reasonable thing.

In 2008, Anita Heiss and Peter Minter published *The Macquarie PEN Anthology of Aboriginal Literature* (Allen & Unwin). I hope they publish another one soon. The anthology ran from the English language writings of David Unaipon to my own first book, *Swallow the Air*, published by UQP in 2006.

It was, will always be, a great honour to be included in that anthology, but we need to revisit its project again. So much has happened since then. We need to shine a light on our oldest stories and our current custodians, our most recent ground-breaking works and others that are still on the horizon – our remote stories and our urban dreamings. That way I could answer that woman in the audience in Canberra, tell her about the novels and the non-fiction, the poetry, the children's books and young adult novels that are there for her to read.

I'd like her and others to learn about our ancestors, too – those who first wore down the road we all traverse, from the late matriarch of the First Nations Australia Writers Network, Kerry-Reed Gilbert, to William Russell 'Werriberrie', King Billy of Appin – who penned *My Recollections* in 1914 and inserted a dictionary of his own in the appendix – and on to Melissa Lucashenko and beyond. In the very act of writing all these stories these writers have sustained us and given all readers, all Australians new and old, a historical record of the life and times of an entire nation. How we aren't to be missed, not anymore.

We have so much to tell you.

Here is our story, the one we carry on our backs with every book we publish, every day and night: the history that never has and never will escape us.

We are your original storytellers. Our culture has survived through story and we are the civilisation with songlines etched in the land you inhabit.

A week after that festival in Canberra, I heard the great writer Tony Birch speak in Melbourne. He said, 'When white people write about Indigenous people, afterwards they can walk away. For us it's a lived experience. With that comes responsibility and accountability.'

This is the history and the story of our accountability and responsibility. It's yours to read too; yours to be responsible and accountable to. I invite you to decolonise your shelf.

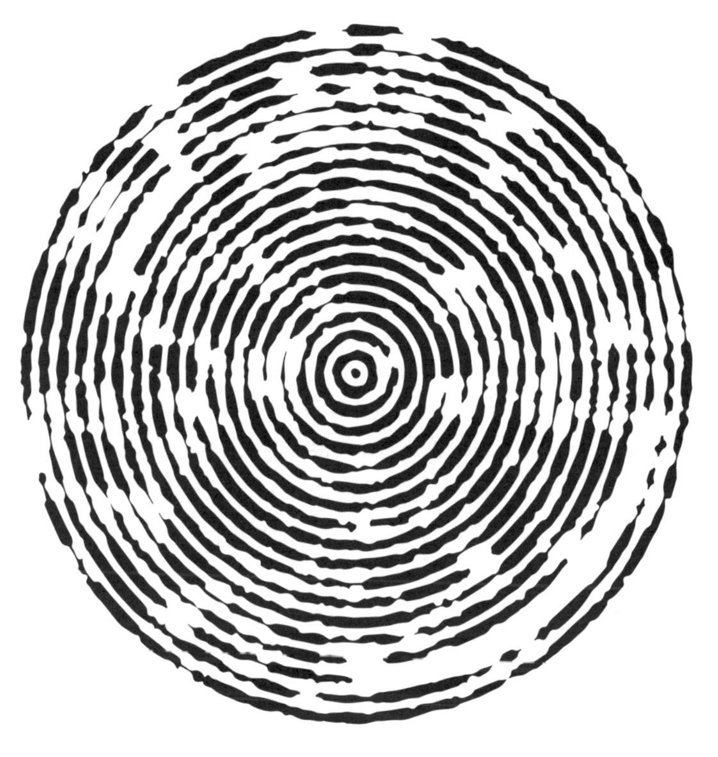

WUURRI-LAY

Amy Thunig

DR AMY THUNIG is a Gomeroi person who parents and partners on beautiful Awabakal Country. A research fellow within Jumbunna at the University of Technology Sydney, Amy's area of expertise is formal education systems and structures within so-called Australia. Amy's first book, *Tell Me Again: A memoir*, was published by UQP and shortlisted in the 2023 Victorian Premier's Literary Awards and the Australian Book Industry Awards. A director at Story Factory in Redfern, Amy contributes on various committees and councils, and is a media commentator and panellist.

My father lives within the rissoles when I cook, his pride bubbling in the gravy made just so. My grandfather sings to me from the sizzle of the pan, the scent of slightly burnt meat and childhood memory filling my home. My mother is a waft of Flex shampoo – she greets me from the tumble of dark hair on my child's shoulders as their towel hits the laundry basket. My grandmothers are woven wool and raffia – they watch over me from walls, hold mementos in baskets, and are draped across bassinets of babies still to come. The heart of my community crackles in the fire of the walaay (camp), warming the aunts in the evening and browning the toast for the gaayili (children) in the morning. What will I be in my own great-grandchildren's worlds? From where and when will I whisper to them when my body is no longer earthside?

We are energy, cells and stardust woven together since time immemorial and that is an understanding that brings more than just beauty – it brings obligation and responsibility, it prompts conscious decisions and intentional hands. It brings to mind wuurri-lay, a word that in Gamilaraay speaks of reciprocity and giving.

Wuurri-lay
'Wuurri' (to give) – 'lay' (reciprocally)

To give to each other reciprocally requires conscious thought and intentional action. Reciprocity is more than just a returning – it may be transferring and transforming, binding, connecting and felt. Within my communities, from my family extending outwards, reciprocity has always been taught to me as being at the forefront of how we should behave and think. If you are offered something and you take it, you should be willing and able to return it when and where you can. A recipe shared can be a meal made, helping hands in the neighbour's garden means a steady supply of lemons.

It is a lesson taught to children at the dinner table about how to behave on the playground. My parents and grandparents told me, 'If someone hits you, always hit them back twice as hard.' This message is both instruction and word of warning; it tells you how to respond if you did not initiate the exchange, but it also warns you of how others may respond if you are the one to throw that first hit. Do not dish out what you aren't prepared to receive doubled.

In adulthood, and beyond the playground, I reflect that such teachings apply not only to physical movements but also to emotions, the holding of space, trust, integrity, and the gathering of storying and knowledge. Treat others how you wish to be treated, and generally that which you give will be brought back to you in some form. Our interactions with people, kin creatures and Country are exchanges of time, energy, sustenance, and may at times be an act of reciprocal harm or healing.

The longer I am in this body the more I understand, with reciprocity in mind, sometimes it is best to simply refuse an offering – not all offered is genuine or worthwhile. 'No response is a response' is a popular adage that comes to mind. Turn off the email notifications, decline the invitation, reconsider what you listen to and honour with your time.

Within the academy I observe that reciprocity is readily promised, but rarely honoured. Non-Indigenous researchers make promises of reciprocity within their ethics proposals, grants and the emails they send blak academics asking to 'pick your brain'. They promise to return whatever they gather in kind, but in my experience the taking of Indigenous time, energy, storying, knowledge, intellectual property is rarely returned or honoured appropriately to such hands. And for those approached, it costs them double: first in the giving; and second in the disappointment of seeing promises broken.

These lessons work within my mind, pour out into my parenting and partnering, and guide my responses more as I move through this life. While energy may be eternal, our existence within these bodies is not. We have here together the briefest of moments, and these moments are precious. It is wuurri-lay that guides my behaviour in the academy, my hands in my community and my heart within my home. If I consider reciprocity, I am more likely to turn my attention to the weaving that awaits me on the couch and the children ready to nestle in beside me. I pour into my family and community and go to sleep wondering if one day I will be remembered in the scent of a favoured jasmine perfume, the taste of a meal made just so, or the sound of the fire crackling.

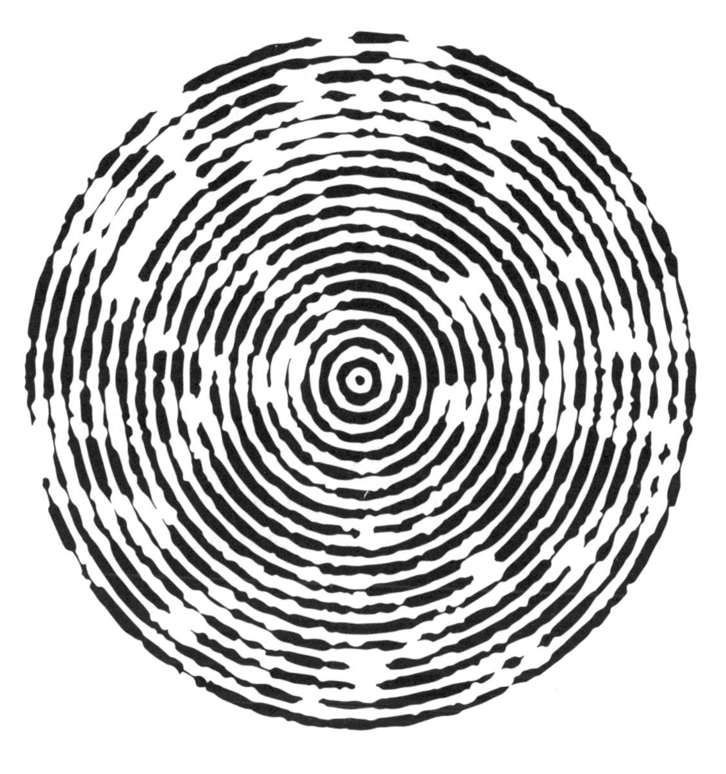

HELD WITHOUT WORDS

Timmah Ball

TIMMAH BALL is a writer, editor and zine-maker of Ballardong Noongar heritage. In 2022 she published the chapbook *Do Planners Dreams of Electric Trees?*, which was developed through an Arts House Residency. She has also contributed to a range of anthologies, such as *This All Come Back Now* and *Best Australian Poems 2022*.

My notebook contains (sounds)
That can't be written
Held without words

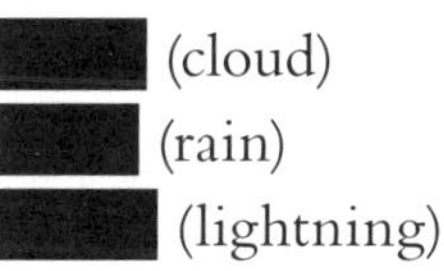

Translated into Dutch
Then Portuguese
Then English –

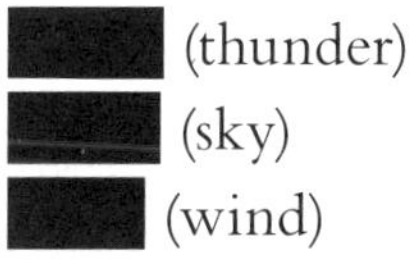

Our words
Without context
But always in place

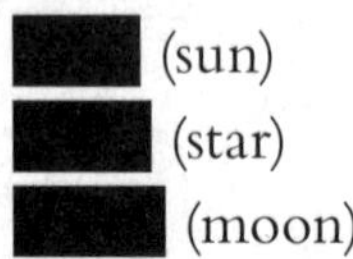

Can you learn Noongar when it is held within other languages? Languages that privilege the written word. People ask about the different spellings of Noongar/ Nyungar, Nyoongar, Nyoongah, Nyungah, Nyugah, Yungar and Noonga. Isn't it obvious? It was transcribed into colonial languages when settlers crudely documented spoken words with foreign alphabets. Noongar dictionaries weren't written by Noongars, but spoken languages will keep being spoken.

About The Poet's Voice

The Poet's Voice believes in the power of collective listening. Working in partnership with festivals and cultural organisations, it has curated large-scale events in beautiful venues, bringing people together to listen to poetry and prose on themes and topics both political and poetic. Whether new Australian interpretations of Dante's *Purgatorio*, a focus on Anna Akhmatova (the beloved poet of Stalin's Russia), or individuals reading from and describing their 'necessary poet', The Poet's Voice strives to show that words shared bring us closer together.

This collaboration with UQP and Jasmin McGaughey comes out of two extraordinary events of listening – at The Wheeler Centre for Books, Writing & Ideas in Melbourne and the National Museum of Australia in Canberra – where First Nations speakers shared words unique and special to them, in language. We are grateful that this book has now enlarged and extended those moments.

Ellen Koshland and Nikki Anderson

www.thepoetsvoice.com.au

Notes

Some pieces from this anthology were previously published in the following places, or were written with consultation and/or permission, as noted.

Anita Heiss's piece was first published online as 'Ngumambinya: trust for help' by *Griffith Review*, Issue 67, 2020.

Ellen van Neerven's piece was first commissioned and published as 'Gibam Garandalehn (Full Moon)' by *Red Room Poetry*. It was also published in the English language in *Guwaya – For All Times* (Magabala Books, 2020).

Elizabeth Ellis's piece was first published online as a transcript of the 'Word for Word – Songlines' interview at the National Museum of Australia in 2018.

Jeanine Leane's piece was first commissioned and published as 'Nginha-gulia nyiang – These Words' by *Red Room Poetry*. It was also published in the English language in *Guwaya – For All Times* (Magabala Books, 2020) and in *Gawimarra: Gathering* (UQP, 2024).

Kim Scott's piece was first published as a transcript of the Ray Mathew Lecture that he delivered as a speech at the National Library of Australia in 2017.

Evelyn Araluen's piece was first published in *Overland*, Issue 223 Winter, 2016; and in *Dropbear* (UQP, 2021).

Tara June Winch's piece was first published online as 'Decolonising the Shelf' by *Griffith Review*, Issue 66, 2019.